MEN PLANNING

FOR

MARRIAGE

© 2014   Patrick J. Hession   Second Edition

All rights reserved

No part of this book may be reproduced, stored in a retrieval system, or transmitted by any means, electronic, mechanical, photocopying, recording, or otherwise, without the written permission of the author.

ISBN: 978-0-6152-1052-0

Cover photo by the author

DISCLAIMER: I am primarily an Educator. Over a period of 25 years of teaching Human Relations, Psychology, and Sociology and through extensive reading, I have complied and adapted the material contained herein. I have made every effort to give proper attribution to the various authors when possible. I do not intend to profit materially from their contributions and ideas but have included them only in furtherance of the concepts related to this workbook.

Books by the author

WORDSEEDS FROM THE WILDERNESS: Calling God's People To Reconciliation, Healing, and Restoration
RECONCILIATION, HEALING, AND RESTORATION OF THE CHURCH
GOD IS YOUR FAMILY: A Key To Your True Identity And Self-Worth
INTIMATE PRAYER
PREPARING THE ARMY OF GOD: A Basic Training Manual For Spiritual Warfare
CHRISTIAN HOMEBUILDING FOR MEN
CHRISTIAN HOMEBUILDING FOR WOMEN
MEN - PLANNING FOR MARRIAGE
WOMEN - PLANNING FOR MARRIAGE

The author can be contacted at familytofamilies@hotmail.com

TABLE OF CONTENTS
MEN PLANNING FOR MARRIAGE

CHAPTER I - ON WHAT FOUNDATION? — 1

- On What Foundation? — 1
- An Invitation To Commit Or Recommit Yourself to Jesus Christ — 3
- Taking Responsibility for Yourself and Your Actions — 6
- Spiritual Gifts and Abilities — 10
- Understanding Yourself — 12
- Stress Analysis — 14
- The Burnout Checklist — 16
- Self-Confidence Assessment — 17
- Self-Disclosure Questionnaire — 20
- Discovering Your Needs — 21
- The Parent, Adult, and Child in You — 25
- Truths That Will Set You Free — 25
- Seven Foundations for a Healthy Self-Image in Christ — 26
- I Am What I Value — 27
- Being Honest with God, Yourself, and Others — 28
- Motivation and Satisfaction — 29
- Goal-Setting with The Lord — 29
- Goal-Setting – Potential Husbands/Fathers — 30
- Your Board of Directors — 31
- Readings
  - Toward a Healthy Sexuality — 32
  - Sexual Fulfillment — 36
  - Cohabitation or "Rent-A-Spouse" — 39
  - Consider the Mother of Jesus — 41

CHAPTER II - GOD'S ORDER FOR THE FAMILY — 44

- God's Order for the Family — 44
- Principles for Making New Friends and Finding a Potential Mate — 44
- Responsibilities toward One Another — 50
- Some Important Questions To Help You Prepare for Marriage — 51
- Christian Principles for a Strong and Enduring Marriage — 54
- Enhancing Your Chances for an Enduring and Happy Marriage — 55
- Conflict Areas That Need To Be Settled in Marriage — 57
- Understanding Your Potential Mate — 57
- Potential Wife's Family Evaluation — 60
- Readings
  - Other Important Activities To Complete — 62
  - Using Your Engagement Productively — 64
  - Marriage — 67
  - Parents Are Called To Witness to Their Faith and Hope — 72
  - Children Have the Right to a Home Like That of Nazareth — 76

The Family and the Good News	79
Christian Family: Witness to the Paschal Covenant	80
The Family: Heart of Evangelization	81
The Christian Family: The Domestic Church	83
The Holiness of the Family at the Service of the Gospel	84
The Eucharist: Sign and Nourishment for Unconditional Love	85
Reconciliation and Forgiveness in the Family	86
The Family: A Community of Prayer	87
The Family: Nucleus and Source of Social Good	88
The Famly and Love for the Weakest	89
The Family: Sanctuary of Life	90
The Family Prepares and Follows Young Families	92

CHAPTER III - THE CHRISTIAN FAMILY - LEADERSHIP OF LOVE — 92

How To Love Your Potential Wife	92
Your Position As A Potential Husband-Father	96
Personal Evaluation For Potential Husbands	101
Readings	
Church Teaching on the Sanctity of Life	106
Abortion, In Vitro Fertilization, and Other Abberations	111
The Natural Family Planning Challenge	121

CHAPTER IV - KIDS AND THEIR TRAINING — 127

Responsibilities toward Your Potential Children	127
Discipline	127
Raising Children Who Can Change the World	129
Parenting Styles and Effective Parent Leadership Skills	131
The Stages of Growth	134
Introducing Your Little Ones to God and to Religion	137
Parents' Expectation Form	139
Child's Expectation Form	140
God's Word to Children and Youth	141
Readings	
Developmental Stages	142
The Limits of Parenthood	146

CHAPTER V - CLEANING OUT THE COBWEBS — 149

Sins That Defile	151
A Celebration of Reconciliation	151

INTIMACY

GENTLY FALLS THE SNOW

DEEP LOVE FLOWS 'TWEEN SOUL AND SOUL

TWO HEARTS BECOME ONE

--Patrick J. Hession

CHAPTER I

ON WHAT FOUNDATION?

"Can mortals be righteous before God? Can human beings be pure before their Maker? Even in his servants he puts no trust, and his angels he charges with error. How much more those who live in houses of clay, whose foundation is in the dust, who are crushed like a moth." (1)

"Will you keep the old way that the wicked have trod? They were snatched away before their time, their foundation was washed away by a flood. They said to God, 'Leave us alone,' and 'What can the Almighty do to us?'" (2)

No! Rather, realize that "you were ransomed from the futile ways inherited from your ancestors, not with perishable things like silver or gold but with the precious Blood of Christ, like that of a lamb without defect or blemish. He was destined before the foundation of the world but was revealed at the end of the ages for your sake." (3) Of him the Lord said, "See, I am laying in Zion a foundation stone, a tested stone, a precious cornerstone, a sure foundation: 'One who trusts will not panic.'" (4)

Indeed, God "chose us in Christ before the foundation of the world to be holy and blameless before him in love. He destined us for adoption as his children through Jesus Christ according to the good pleasure of his will. In him, we have redemption through his Blood, the forgiveness of our trespasses and transgressions, according to the riches of his grace that he lavished on us. In him, you also, when you had heard the word of truth, the Gospel of your salvation, and had believed in him, were marked with the seal of the promised Holy Spirit. This is the pledge of our inheritance toward redemption as God's own people to the praise of his glory." (5) "Through him you have come to trust in God, who raised him from the dead and gave him glory so that your faith and hope are set on God." (6)

"God's firm foundation stands, bearing this inscription: 'The Lord knows those who are his,' and 'Let everyone who calls on the name of the Lord turn away from wickedness.'" (7)

This same Jesus says to you, "I will show you what someone is like who comes to me, hears my words, and acts on them. That one is like a man building a house, who dug deeply and laid the foundation on rock. When a flood arose, the river burst against that house but could not shake it because it had been well built. The one who hears and does not act is like a man who built a house on the ground without a foundation. When the river burst against it, immediately it fell, and great was the ruin of that house." (8)

You, therefore, must be careful how you build. "No one can lay any foundation other the one that has been laid. That foundation is Jesus Christ. If anyone builds on the foundation with gold, silver, precious stones, wood, hay, straw - the work of each builder will become visible. The Day (of Judgment) will disclose it because it will be revealed with fire, and the fire will test what sort of work each has done. If what has been built on the foundation survives, the builder will receive a reward. If the work is burned up, the builder will suffer loss. The builder will be saved, but only as through fire." (9)

To sum up, then, if Jesus Christ is not the foundation of your personal house (your personal life), he will not be the foundation of your marriage or of your family. Therefore, "Revere the Lord and serve him in sincerity and in faithfulness. Put away the gods that your ancestors served. If you are unwilling to serve the Lord, choose this day whom you will serve." (10)

(1)	Job 4:17-19		(6)	1 Peter 1:21
(2)	Job 22:15-17		(7)	2 Timothy 2:19
(3)	1 Peter 1:18-20		(8)	Luke 6:47-49
(4)	Isaiah 28:16		(9)	1 Corinthians 3:11-15
(5)	Ephesians 1:4 & 5, 7 & 8, 11-1		(10)	Joshua 23:14 & 15

AN INVITATION TO COMMIT OR RE-COMMIT YOURSELF TO JESUS CHRIST

1. Jesus says to you, "No one can see the kingdom of God without being born from above (by God the Father). No one can enter the kingdom of God without being born of water and Spirit. What is born of the flesh (human nature) is flesh and what is born of the Spirit is spirit" (John 3:3, 5 & 6).

> Have you been born from above by God the Father through the Holy Spirit and Baptism?
>
> YES ( )   NO ( )   I DON'T KNOW ( )

2. God so loved you that he gave his only Son so that, if you believe in him, you may not perish but may have eternal life. God did not send his Son into the world to condemn you but to save you. If you believe in him, you are not condemned. I you do not believe, you are condemned already because you have not believed in the Name of the only Son of God. If you believe and are baptized, you will be saved. If you do not believe, you will be condemned (John 3:16-18; Mark 16:16).

> Even though you may have been baptized or even may have attended church most of your life, can you remember a time in your life when you deliberately repented of your sins and made a personal profession of faith in and acceptance of Jesus as your Savior and Lord from your heart?
>
> YES ( )   NO ( )   I'M NOT SURE ( )

3. If you believe in the Son, you have eternal life. If you disobey the Son, you will not see life but must endure God's wrath. Jesus says, "I am the gate for the sheep. All who came before me are thieves and bandits, but the sheep did not listen to them. I am the gate. Whoever enters through me will be saved and will come and go out and find pasture. The thief comes only to steal and kill and destroy; I came so that they may have life and have it abundantly" (John 3:36; 10:7-10).

> Have you ever surrendered your will completely to God and committed your life to the lordship and authority of Jesus Christ to follow him whatever the cost?
>
> YES ( )   NO ( )   OFF AND ON ( )

4. Jesus says, "Come to me, you who are weary and are carrying heavy burdens, and I will give you rest. Take my yoke upon you and learn from me for I am gentle and humble in heart. You will find rest for your soul. My yoke is easy and my burden is light." "I appeal to you, therefore, brothers and sisters, by the mercies of God, to present your body as a living sacrifice, holy andacceptable to God, which is your spiritual worship. Do not be conformed to this world but be transformed by the renewing of your mind so that you may discern what is the will of God, what is good and acceptable and perfect." Jesus says again, "Listen, I am standing at the door, knocking. If you hear my voice and open the door, I will come in to you and eat with you, and you with me. To the one who conquers, I will give a place with me on my throne, just as I

myself conquered and sat down with my Father on his throne" (Matthew 11:28-30; Romans 121:1 & 2; Revelation 3:20 & 21).

> Are you willing to commit or to re-commit yourself to Jesus Christ as the only true foundation of your life and to let him empower you by his Holy Spirit to be what he has called you to be from all eternity?
>
> YES ( )   NO ( )

As an acceptance of this invitation, pray the prayer of surrender that follows. It may not all apply to you, but make it your own where it does.

PRAYER OF SURRENDER

Jesus, I acknowledge that I was born in a condition of separation from God because of the Original Sin of disobedience by our first parents and am, therefore, a sinner by nature and by choice. In your Word, the Scriptures, you have said that "it is from within, from the human heart, that evil intentions come: fornication, theft, murder, adultery, greed, wickedness, deceit, licentiousness, envy, slander, pride, folly, impurity, idolatry, sorcery, enmities, strife, jealousy, anger, quarrels, dissensions, factions, drunkenness, carousing, and things like these. All these evil things come from within, and they defile a person" (Mark 7:20-23; Galatians 5:19-21).

No wonder my life is such a mess! It is full of many of those things, and I have been content to do nothing about them. But, Jesus, you took all these upon yourself and died on the Cross, even though you were never guilty of any of them yourself. By your death on the Cross you bridged the gulf between man and God. You became the bridge over which I can cross from death to life and thus be reconciled with the Father. You desire to save me from this human nature and from eternal damnation. You want to give me, instead, a share in your divine nature.

Jesus, I am tired of going nowhere. I acknowledge that I am really not in control of my life at all. I have been letting all these things you said are part of my human nature control me. I confess, Lord, and agree with you that I have not made much of my life to this point.

Jesus, I am truly sotry for and regret my sins. I turn away from my sinful nature and life. I turn around from the direction I have been going and ask your forgiveness for my stubbornness and my unwillingness to let you be Savior and Lord. Jesus, have mercy on me and forgive me, a sinner!

I give up my struggle to be somebody when, in reality, I now realize that I am nothing apart from you. I surrender to you, Jesus, and to your perfect plan for my life. I receive and accept you as my Savior and Lord. Bring me to friendship with your Father so that I can know him as my Father also.

Fill me with the abundant life for which you died and rose from the dead. Make me the new creation that you want me to be (1 Corinthians 5:17 & 18). Fill me with new life and power through your Holy Spirit whom you and the Father have sent and through whom I also can say, "Abba, my Father, my Daddy".

Bring forth in me the fruit of your Spirit: the fruit of love, of joy, of peace, of patience, of kindness, of generosity, of faithfulness, of gentleness, of self control (Galatians 5:22 & 23),

Thank you, Lord Jesus. And, when I slip back into one of the sins of my old human nature, which I will at times, help me turn quickly to you and ask your forgiveness because you have promised to forgive me if only I confess my sins, express my sorrow and regret for them because they offend you, turn away from them, and turn back to you (1 John 1:9).

TAKING RESPONSIBILITY FOR YOURSELF AND YOUR ACTIONS

You are always in relationship with someone: with God, with your family members, with others at church or on the job. You are influenced, and influence others, by the quality of your relationships. And, you are responsible to God and to others for the quality of your relationships.

The degree of satisfaction you have with your personal life will have a positive or negative effect on all of your other relationships. You can only "love your neighbor as yourself" to the degree that you properly love yourself. You can only love yourself properly to the extent that you understand and accept God's love for you and the relationship with him to which he calls you.

The starting point, therefore, in effective relationships with others is the relationship you have with yourself. You must first understand yourself and learn to deal effectively with yourself. To the degree that you take responsibility for yourself and your actions, to that degree will you be freed up to help and to love others.

Four useful methods to gain self-understanding are:

- ➢ Acquire general information about human behavior and apply it to yourself.
- ➢ Listen to what others say about you or to you.
- ➢ Obtain feedback from self-examination exercises.
- ➢ See what God's Word has to say about you and ask God to help you see yourself as he sees you.

As you work through this material, you will be exploring aspects of human behavior. Consider seriously those aspects that you believe apply to you or that can be helpful to your personal and spiritual growth and development. What you learn that you already know can be a source of encouragement to you. Confirmation and affirmation are sometimes as important as information. Some things you may find do not apply to you and to your situation, at least not at the present time.

One caution: it is possible to become too introspective. Feedback that you receive from others who love you and whom you trust can help you keep your balance. Feedback from self-examination exercises may provide valuable clues to your preferences, values, and personal characteristics. While they are not intended to be scientific, they can provide useful information about you. This depends, however, on the extent to which you are honest with yourself.

The most important way to build strong self-respect is to understand how God sees and accepts you. The more aware you become of how God loves and accepts you in spite of your sinfulness and imperfections, the more you can accept yourself.

When you accept yourself for who you are in God's eyes and do not reject yourself, you can develop a healthy self-concept. You will, then, be able to regard others more highly. One way to improve your self-acceptance is to be willing to disclose more of yourself to God and to others. Another way is to develop an appreciation of the gifts and talents that God has given to you. This will lead to a greater sense of personal satisfaction.

Personal satisfaction refers to accepting yourself for who you are and enjoying what you are doing. It is extremely hard to get anywhere in life unless you can get along well with yourself and with other people.

People are often overlooked because they give the impression that they cannot handle responsibility for themselves or for others. The most important skills for success, properly understood, are the interpersonal skills that are necessary for cooperating with others in your family, church, job, and social life. To achieve this, you must make a deliberate, free will decision to let God help you change your behavior as needed to make you successful for him. The following suggestions may help you.

Be Real With God - Look at yourself honestly. Ask him to show you yourself as he sees you. In order to plan and to grow properly, you need an honest picture of your strengths, areas for improvement, goals, and values. You will be taking a look at these shortly.

Don't Stand Out In The Wrong Way - While maintaining your liberty as a child of God, you need to be conventional in your behavior. This means maintaining the legitimate and customary dress, manners, and customs of the society or organization within which you live and work. Keep in mind that you are to be a reflection and an extension of God, your Father, and Jesus, your Brother. Being all things to all men means drawing attention ultimately to God, not to yourself.

Conventional behavior includes such things as good manners, politeness, respect for and obedience to legitimate authority, good attendance and punctuality at home, at church, and on the job, careful grooming, good posture, and adherence to reasonable rules and laws. Your clothing and speech should project one who understands who he or she is in Christ. Your standard of dress should be modest and appropriate to the situation.

Be Content - Learn to become content where you are. Parents will not long tolerate the ranting and complaining of discontented, spoiled brats. Neither will God! Accept that God has you where you are right now either because he is trying to teach you something or because he wants to work through you there. Accepting reality requires the realization that it takes a certain amount of time and experience before you are promoted on a job or before the Lord can use you effectively in another situation. Learning to be content with much or with little, whether in finances, prestige, or position, is an essential requirement for God to be able to use you according to his plan for you.

Apply What You Learn - Another aspect of reality that causes problems for many people is resistance to the application of knowledge. Wisdom is the ability to apply knowledge in particular situations. It is a common perception of our society today that education and science are the solutions to all of humankind's problems. A variation of this in Christian circles is that "knowledge of the Word," or Bible study, is what is needed. Both of these approaches are only part of reality.

Jesus makes it perfectly clear that we are to be *doers* of the Word, not hearers only. Jesus taught that it is not those who *say* "Lord, Lord" but those who *do* the will of the Father who are truly his followers. Scripture tells us that the demons in Hell believe and even tremble.

It is evident that education or knowledge alone is not enough. Knowledge, infused with wisdom from God, leads to works of faith as well as to effective and constructive action.

Again, this requires prayer, patience to wait on God's timing, and application of interpersonal skills. Action directed to bringing about constructive change in particular takes time. In situations like this, you must learn to accept the reality that an idea that may seem sound to you must still be accepted by other people. God, by his Spirit, must direct you as to how and when to bring this about.

Be Loyal and Honest - Being loyal and honest in all of your relationships and dealings with others means keeping in mind the best interest of your family, church, or workplace. You must learn to prefer others before yourself. A loyal person does not complain about or take part in gripe sessions about his or her spouse, children, church, or place of employment. He or she will emphasize the good aspects of these to the community. Being loyal, however, does not mean that you surrender your ability to make constructive criticism about things that need to be changed.

Be Determined and Confident - Spiritual growth and development are *your* responsibility. You are to work out your salvation in the fear of the Lord. You should remember that much of the self-development that you need happens outside of a book or retreat.

Prayer, Bible study, and spiritual reading are important sources of spiritual growth. But, the ultimate strategy for spiritual development is to believe in who you are in Christ and in what you are doing and to persist in doing it. Eventually, your contributions will be recognized because what you are doing is worthwhile and valuable.

It is important to remember and to remind yourself that God has gifted you with particular talents and abilities and that he wants and expects you to develop and to use these for his glory and for building up his kingdom on earth. He wants you to be successful!

The ultimate solution for developing self-confidence is to see yourself as God sees you, redeemed and restored as his child through his Son, Jesus Christ. The greatest confidence-builder is the realization that you are important to God and that he needs and depends on you to use your gifts in line with his plan for your life.

Effective self-confidence and leadership develop as you seriously seek and accept God's lordship and leadership over you and as you then move in his timing to do those things that he has in mind for you to do. Raise your spiritual sights and believe that you can do all things through Christ who strengthens you.

Another set of suggestions centers around taking control of your environment or at least adapting it to your advantage. Included here are the following:

Stay Tuned to What Is Going On around You in Your Family, Church, and World - Awareness of the world around you keeps you from becoming self-centered, helps you head off problems before they become serious, and provides opportunities for ministry and intercessory prayer. Even though you are not *of* the world, you are very much *in* it and are to minister the love and life of Jesus *to* it.

Develop a Plan of Prayer and Bible Study - Planning your Bible study involves seeking to discover and to carry out God's plan for you. He will often speak to you as you read his Word and as you talk to him in prayer. Study to show yourself approved.

Acquire Broad Experience - Many people whom God uses are people of broad experience. Therefore, a widely accepted suggestion for advancing in service and responsibility is to make yourself available in several areas. Begin at home, then in the church. The home is your *primary* training ground for service in the Church. Don't seek the highest place at the table, however, but, as a servant, be willing to take the lowest place and let the Lord promote you. If you would be the greatest, learn to be the servant of all.

Broadening your experience can come about by performing a variety of services or sometimes by performing essentially the same service in different situations. You can also obtain breadth by serving on committees and by undertaking special assignments.

Find a Good Spiritual Leader or Mentor - A very important safeguard to proper spiritual development is to find someone whom you can respect and to follow and learn all that you can from him or her. Be very careful, however, that he or she is truly following Jesus Christ.

Take Advantage of Opportunities - Recognize opportunities and be ready to accept new responsibilities as the Lord brings them across your path. If you maintain a record of excellent service and availability, you will be in a position to be used in greater service.

SPIRITUAL GIFTS AND ABILITIES

We have gifts that differ according to the favor bestowed on each of us. You are to use your gifts in accordance with the grace that God has given you. Do not think of yourself more highly than you should. Instead, be modest in your thinking and judge yourself according to the amount of faith that God has given you. As a generous distributor of God's manifold grace, put your gift at the service of others in the measure that you have received (Romans 12:8; 12:3; 1 Peter 4:10).

Ask God to reveal the particular gift(s) he has given to you. Check off those that he shows you.

___Wisdom in discourse, or the ability to give a word or a message that is full of wisdom (1 Corinthians 12:8).

___The power to express knowledge, or the ability to give a word or message that is full of knowledge (1 Corinthians 12:8).

___Faith in particular circumstances to do what seems to be impossible (! Corinthians 12:9).

___The gift of healing, or the power to heal (1 Corinthians 12:9).

___Miraculous powers, or the power to work miracles (1 Corinthians 12:10).

___The gift of speaking God's message in prophecy; its use should be proportion to your faith (Romans 12:5; 1 Corinthians 12:10).

___The power to distinguish one spirit from another, or the ability to tell the difference between gifts that come from the Spirit of God and those that do not (1 Corinthians 12:10).

___The gift of tongues, or the ability to speak or to pray in an unknown tongue or language (1 Corinthians 12:10; 12:28).

___The gift of interpreting tongues or to explain what is said (1 Corinthians 12:10).

___The gift of ministry or service; it should be used to serve others. The one who serves is to do it with the strength provided by God (Romans 12:7; 1 Peter 4:11).

___Teaching; one who is a teacher should use one's gift for teaching (Romans 12:8).

___The power to exhort, or the gift of encouraging others (Romans 12:8).

___Giving money or sharing resources with others; it should be done generously (Romans 12:8).

___Ruling or exercising authority; one should work hard and exercise authority with care (Romans 12:8).

___Performing works of mercy, or showing kindness to others (1 Corinthians 12:8).

___Helpers, or those who have the ability to help others (1 Corinthians 12:18).

___Administrators, or those who have the ability to direct others (1 Corinthians 12:28)

___Hospitality to strangers, for some have entertained angels without knowing it (Hebrews 13:2).

___Concern for those in prison, as though in prison with them (Hebrews 12:3).

___Concern for those who are badly treated (Hebrews 13:3).

UNDERSTANDING YOURSELF

Whether you consciously know it or not, your beliefs, attitudes, and things you say or do (behaviors) have been influenced to a significant degree, for good or for bad, by your parents or step-parents, or lack thereof.

They were your first and most important teachers and role-models of what a man or woman should be or do. Just as you often bear a physical resemblance to one or both of your parents, so also your psychological and spiritual development, or lack of it, will also reflect your upbringing. Their influence likewise colors your definition of yourself as a man or a woman.

You say and do what you do because that is the way you were taught. If you don't learn other, perhaps better, ways of speaking and doing things, there is no reason or basis for change.

Now, while boys and girls are influenced by *both* parents, they tend to be influenced more by the parent of the same sex, especially in their most formative and impressionable years (your first 5-7 years). This is because, positively or negatively, your father (step-father) or mother (step-mother) becomes your role model of the man or woman you would become when you grew up into adulthood.

Even if you discover and try to follow other "role models," your earliest formation by your "parent" figures remains the strongest influence on you. But, if you can begin to understand their influences on you, you can *choose* to change those things in you that you don't like in yourself. This may take the help of a trained counselor or spiritual leader, and you should remain open to this help. This is one of the important reasons for discipleship.

The following questions will help you bring to consciousness some of those beliefs, attitudes, and behaviors and how they have influenced your self-concept and self-esteem. Answer the questions for the parent or step-parent who was most influential during your first 5-7 years.

Your Father (Step-Father)

1. What does (did) your father (step-father) think about women?

2. How are (were) girls and women treated in your family?

3. Does (did) your father (step-father) compliment your mother (step-mother)?   YES ( )   NO ( )   NOT VERY OFTEN ( )

4. Is (was) your father (step-father) affectionate with her?   YES ( )   NO ( )   NOT VERY OFTEN ( )

5. Does (did) your father (step-father) still seem to be in love with your mother (step-mother)?
YES ( )   NO ( )   HE DOESN'T SHOW IT ( )

6. Does (did) he treat her as an equal?   YES ( )   NO ( )

7. Does (did) he respect her intelligence?   YES ( )   NO ( )

8. Does (did) she have a part in major family decisions?   YES ( )   NO ( )

9. Is (was) he involved with his children?   YES ( )   NO ( )   With you specifically?   YES ( )   NO ( )

10. Does (did) he provide well for his family?   YES ( )   NO ( )   AS WELL AS HE WAS ABLE ( )

11. Is (was) he ambitious?   YES ( )   NO ( )

12. Is (was) he the spiritual leader for his family?   YES ( )   NO ( )

13. Does (did) he abuse alcohol or other drugs, including prescription drugs?   YES ( )   NO ( )

14. Does (did) he abuse you physically?   YES ( )   NO ( )   emotionally?   YES ( )   NO ( )   sexually?   YES ( )   NO ( )

15. Are (were) you close to your father (step-father) in a healthy way?   YES ( )   NO ( )   MODERATELY ( )

16. Is (was) your relationship with your father (step-father) happy?   YES ( )   NO ( )   MODERATELY ( )

17. Have you forgiven your father (step-father) for anything he may have done to or against you whether intentionally or not?   YES ( )   NO ( )

Your Mother (Step-Mother)

1. What does (did) your mother (step-mother) think about men?

2. How are (were) boys treated in your family?

3. Does (did) your mother (step-mother) compliment your father (step-father)?   YES ( )   NO ( )   NOT VERY OFTEN ( )

4. Is (was) your mother (step-mother) affectionate with him?   YES ( )   NO ( )   NOT VERY OFTEN ( )

5. Does (did) your mother (step-mother) still seem to be in love with your father (step-father)?
YES ( )   NO ( )   SHE DOESN'T (DIDN'T) SHOW IT ( )

6. Does (did) your mother (step-mother) still make herself attractive to your father (step-father)?
YES ( )   NO ( )

7. Does (did) your mother (step-mother) admire and respect your father (step-father)?   YES ( )   NO ( )

8. Does (did) she respect his leadership?   YES ( )   NO ( )

9. Does (did) she yield when he makes (made) major decisions?   YES ( )   NO ( )   COMPLAININGLY ( )

10. What kind of housekeeper is (was) she?   NEAT ( )   MESSY ( )

11. Is (was) she involved with her children?   YES ( )   NO ( )   With you specifically?   YES ( )   NO ( )

12. How well does (did) she care for her children?   VERY WELL ( )   MODERATELY WELL ( )   AS WELL AS SHE WAS ABLE ( )   POORLY ( )

13. Is (was) she ambitious?   YES ( )   NO ( )

14. Can (could) she cook?   YES ( )   NO ( )   SOMEWHAT ( )

15. Has she continued (did she continue) to develop her mind?   YES ( )   NO ( )

16. Is (was) she a reader?   YES ( )   NO ( )

17. Is (was) she committed to her religious beliefs?   YES ( )   NO ( )

18. Does (did) she abuse alcohol or other drugs, including prescription drugs?   YES ( )   NO ( )

19. Does (did) she abuse you physically?   YES ( )   NO ( )   emotionally?   YES ( )   NO ( )   sexually?   YES ( )   NO ( )

20. Are (were) you close to your mother (step-mother) in a healthy way?   YES ( )   NO ( )   MODERATELY ( )

21. Is (was) your relationship with your mother (step-mother) happy?   YES ( )   NO ( )   MODERATELY ( )

22. Have you forgiven your mother (step-mother) for anything she may have done to or against you whether intentionally or not?   YES ( )   NO ( )

Questionnaire adapted from an interview with Dr. Richard Dobbins in CHARISMA, March, 1986

STRESS ANALYSIS

To roughly estimate if you are experiencing too many negative consequences of stress (or too much distress), apply each question to the last six months of your life. Answer each question mostly yes or mostly no.

	Mostly Yes	Mostly No
1. Have you been feeling uncomfortably tense lately?	_____	_____
2. Are you engaged in frequent arguments with people close to you?	_____	_____
3. Is your romantic life very unsatisfactory?	_____	_____
4. Do you feel lethargic about life?	_____	_____
5. Do you have trouble sleeping?	_____	_____
6. Do many people annoy or irritate you?	_____	_____
7. Do you have constant cravings for candy or other sweets?	_____	_____
8. If you smoke, is your cigarette consumption way up?	_____	_____
9. Are you becoming addicted to soft drinks or coffee?	_____	_____
10. Do you find it difficult to concentrate on your work?	_____	_____
11. Do you frequently grind your teeth?	_____	_____
12. Are you increasingly forgetful about little things like mailing a letter?	_____	_____
13. Are you increasingly forgetful about big things like appointments and major errands?	_____	_____
14. Are you making far too many trips to the bathroom?	_____	_____
15. Have people commented lately that you do not look well?	_____	_____
16. Do you get into verbal fights with other people too frequently?	_____	_____
17. Do you have more than your share of tension headaches?	_____	_____
18. Have you been involved in more than one physical fight lately?	_____	_____

19. Do you feel nauseated much too often?   _____   _____

20. Do you feel light-headed or dizzy almost everyday?   _____   _____

21. Do you have churning sensations in your stomach far too often?   _____   _____

22. Are you in a hurry all the time?   _____   _____

23. Are far too many things bothering you these days?   _____   _____

SCORING: The following guidelines are of value only if you answered the questions sincerely.

0-5   Mostly YES answers: You seem to be experiencing a normal amount of stress.

6-15 Mostly Yes answers: Your stress level seems high. Become involved in some kind of stress management activities.

16-23 Mostly Yes answers: Your stress level appears much too high. Seek the help of a mental health professional, visit your family doctor, or both.

HUMAN RELATIONS FOR CAREER AND PERSONAL SUCCESS, Andrew J. DuBrin, Reston Publishing Company, Inc., 1983, pp. 76 & 77

THE BURNOUT CHECKLIST

Check each one of the following statements that generally applies to you.

_____ 1.   I feel tired much more often than I used to.

_____ 2.   I get very irritated lately.

_____ 3.   I suffer from a number of annoying physical problems such as neck aches and backaches.

_____ 4.   I often feel that I am losing control of my life.

_____ 5.   I am feeling pretty depressed these days.

_____ 6.   I get down on myself too often.

_____ 7.   My life seems to be at a dead end.

_____ 8.   My enthusiasm for life has gone way down.

_____ 9.   I am tired of dealing with the same old problems.

_____ 10. Lately, I have kind of withdrawn from friends and family.

_____ 11. Not much seems funny to me anymore.

_____ 12. There is really nothing for me to look forward to on the job or at school.

_____ 13. It is difficult for me to care about what is going on in the world outside.

_____ 14. My spark is gone.

_____ 15. I know that I have a problem but just don't have the energy to do anything about it.

_____ 16. I can't think of the last time I didn't dread going to work or school.

_____ 17. Friends say that my temper is getting short.

_____ 18. I don't get nearly enough appreciation from my superiors.

_____ 19. I don't see any good alternatives ahead of me for improving my life.

_____ 20. I think I have reached a dead end in life.

_____ TOTAL

Interpretation: The more of these statements that apply to you, the more likely it is that you are experiencing burnout. If you checked 15 or more of these statements, it would be helpful to discuss your feelings with a mental health professional or spiritual leader.

SELF-CONFIDENCE ASSESSMENT

Circle the answer that best applies to you.

A. You are assigned a task involving an entire area that is unfamiliar to you. You would

   1. Delegate someone else to do it.
   2. Get someone to help you do it.
   3. Study the procedure carefully and then do it yourself.
   4. Plunge right into the work without giving it much thought.

B. You solicit the advice of others before making a decision.

   1. Almost always.
   2. Sometimes.
   3. Rarely.
   4. Never.

C. You offer advice to others.

   1. Never.
   2. Hardly ever.
   3. Willingly, if you are asked to do so.
   4. Often, even when no one asks for it.

D. At meetings, you come up with ideas for projects.

   1. Never.
   2. Sometimes.
   3. Frequently.
   4. Always, to let your boss or others know you've got a million ideas.

E. When meeting with your superiors, you acknowledge the ideas you've received from others rather than passing them off as your own.

   1. Never.
   2. Rarely.
   3. Often.
   4. Always.

F. Your boss expresses an opinion that is contrary to your strong beliefs or convictions. You would

   1. Remain silent.
   2. Attempt to disagree only if you believed that it would not jeopardize your job.
   3. Explain your beliefs about the issue.
   4. Become incensed and speak up about your views.

G. If there were an opening that you would like in a higher classification or office, you would

   1. Wait until a superior asked if you were interested in it.
   2. Drop hints that you just might be interested in it.
   3. Go through the regular channels to apply for it.
   4. Do everything you can to persuade your superior that he/she should recommend you for the position.

H. You believe that your work is inadequate.

   1. Always.
   2. Frequently.
   3. Hardly ever.
   4. Never.

I. You believe that you deserve a position of leadership in an organization or in your job.

   1. No.
   2. Perhaps.
   3. Yes, and hope others recognize your leadership qualities.
   4. Without a doubt.

J. You believe that you are brighter than many of your colleagues.

   1. Never.
   2. At times.
   3. Usually.
   4. Of course.

K. In response to criticism, you

   1. Feel devastated and say nothing to the person who made the comment.
   2. Become angry at first, but later try to analyze the criticism.
   3. Discuss the matter with the person who made the comment and try to resolve it.
   4. Tell the person to buzz off.

L. At a party, you introduce yourself to people you don't know and begin conversations.

   1. Never.
   2. Hardly ever.
   3. Usually.
   4. Always.

M. In a restaurant, you will complain about improper service or bad food.

   1. Never.
   2. Sometime
   3. Usually, and in a calm, constructive way.
   4. Always and loudly.

N. While waiting in a long line for a bus or at the movies or supermarket,

   1. You let others get ahead of you.
   2. You wait patiently wherever you my be.
   3. You try to speed up the line.
   4. You push ahead of others.

O. When someone compliments you about something you've done,

   1. You are embarrassed and don't know what to say.
   2. You say, "Oh, it was nothing, really."
   3. You smile and say, "Thank you."
   4. You say, "Thanks," and add, "Yes, I know I'm talented and wonderful."

Score your self by adding up the numbers you checked. If you scored 16-25, you are eating too much humble pie. If you scored 26-35, your self-confidence quotient is not low, but you could work a little on raising your self-esteem. If you scored 35-50, you are brimming with self-confidence. If you scored 51-60, you are an overconfident type who should give some thought to tempering your arrogance.

<u>HUMAN RELATIONS FOR CAREER AND PERSONAL SUCCESS</u>, Andrew J. DuBrin, Reston Publishing Company, Inc., 1983, pp. 312 & 313

THE SELF-DISCLOSURE QUESTIONNAIRE

Directions: The following quiz may indicate how much of yourself you reveal to others. Think about the person closest to you, whether he or she is a parent or close friend. Using the list of responses provided, review the questions and select the number of the response that best describes you.

1. I have not mentioned anything about this.
2. I have talked about this to some degree.
3. I have confided this to a large degree.
4. I have disclosed practically all there is to know about this.

_____ 1. Traits I am ashamed of, such as jealousy, daydreaming, and procrastination.

_____ 2. Pet peeves or prejudices about others.

_____ 3. Facts about my love life, including details about flirting, dating, and sexual activity.

_____ 4. Things I have done or said to others that I feel guilty about.

_____ 5. What it takes to make me extremely angry.

_____ 6. My feelings about my attractiveness and sex appeal, and my insecurities about how my romantic interests perceive me.

_____ 7. Aspects of myself I wish I could improve, such as my figure or physique, mental abilities, shyness.

_____ 8. What I worry about most, such as illness, job loss, death, and so forth.

_____ 9. Impulses I fear will get out of control if I "let go", such as drinking, gambling, sex, and anger.

_____ 10. My very deepest sensitivities, dreams, and goals.

Scoring and Interpretation

To tally your score, add the numbers that correspond with the answers you gave to the quiz questions.

10-17 points: You are a closed person. You may feel satisfied with the level of intimacy you have established with others, but it is likely that you would benefit from sharing your feelings more openly. Doing so allows others to give you feedback on your feelings and goals, helping you to get a clearer picture of yourself. Begin to change your style by making small disclosures at first. Perhaps it will be easier to start by talking about your goals.

18-28 points.: You are average on self-disclosure and have a good balance between your private self and your openness.

29-40 points: You are a very open type of person, but beware. Sometimes revealing too much indiscriminately can be a sign of personal insecurity, guilt, or the need for acceptance by others. If others take advantage of you, look down on you, or feel uncomfortable with you, you may be telling more than the listener wants or cares to handle.

<u>HUMAN RELATIONS FOR CAREER AND PERSONAL SUCCESS</u>, Andrew J. DuBrin, second edition, Prentice-Hall, Inc. 1988, page 15

DISCOVERING YOUR NEEDS

A *need* is a lack of something *required* or *desirable* which, if not met, makes you feel *threatened* or *lacking* as a person. Needs are what motivate you to do or to be something or someone. Some needs are weaker or stronger in different persons and within the same person.

Identify the needs you are trying to satisfy:

- **Spiritual Needs**: need for a relationship or involvement with God the Father, Jesus the Son, and the Holy Spirit.

- **Basic or Physiological Needs**: refer to bodily needs: food, water, shelter, sleep, oxygen, activity, normal body temperature.

- **Safety or Security Needs**: physical as well as emotional: comfort, preparation for the future, self-preservation, safe environment, protection, justice, stability, freedom from threat, want, or injury.

- **Esteem Needs**: sense of self-worth, self-respect, self-identity, dignity, importance, privacy, respect from others, recognition, freedom, status, excellence, power.

- **Actualizing or Creative Needs**: creativity, self-expression, self-fulfillment, use of potential, independence, feeling of usefulness, productivity, achievement

Needs are neither good nor bad but are just part of you. *How* you try to meet your needs may be good (constructive or productive) or bad (limiting or counterproductive). If you know what needs you are trying to meet, with God's help through prayer you can, then, evaluate and choose those behaviors that *best* help you meet those needs and eliminate those behaviors that only *seem* to be meeting your needs.

PERSONAL NEEDS ASSESSMENT

The following statements have seven possible responses.

Strongly Agree	Agree	Slightly Agree	Don't	Slightly Disagree	Disagree	Strongly Disagree
+3	+2	+1	0	-1	-2	-3

Please mark one of the seven responses by circling the number that corresponds to the one that best fits your opinion. For example, if you "Strongly Agree", circle number "+3". Complete every item.

1.	I should receive special financial awards when I do my work well.	+3	+2	+1	0	-1	-2	-3
2.	Better task or work descriptions would be helpful so that I will know exactly what is expected of me.	+3	+2	+1	0	-1	-2	-3
3.	I need to be reminded that how much money I get depends on the ability of the organization or other sources to provide adequately.	+3	+2	+1	0	-1	-2	-3
4.	I need to be assured that the physical conditions in which I live or work are safe.	+3	+2	+1	0	-1	-2	-3
5.	I require a friendly and loving atmosphere in which to live or work.	+3	+2	+1	0	-1	-2	-3
6.	Individual recognition for above standard performance means a lot to me.	+3	+2	+1	0	-1	-2	-3
7.	Indifferent leadership from those over me often causes my feelings to be hurt.	+3	+2	+1	0	-1	-2	-3
8.	I need to feel that my real talents and gifts are recognized and put to use.	+3	+2	+1	0	-1	-2	-3
9.	It is important to me that whatever I do is stimulating and challenging.	+3	+2	+1	0	-1	-2	-3
10.	It is important for me to give my best in everything I do.	+3	+2	+1	0	-1	-2	-3
11.	Outings and other social activities are important to make me feel like I belong.	+3	+2	+1	0	-1	-2	-3
12.	Pride in my accomplishments is an important reward in itself.	+3	+2	+1	0	-1	-1	-3
13.	It is important to me to think of of myself as "the best" at what I do.	+3	+2	+1	0	-1	-2	-3

14.	The quality of my relationships is very important to me.	+3	+2	+1	0	-1	-2	-3
15.	Individual incentive rewards and/or allowances would help me improve my performance or behavior.	+3	+2	+1	0	-1	-2	-3
16.	It is important for me to be seen with important people.	+3	+2	+1	0	-1	-2	-3
17.	It is important for me to schedule what I do and to make my own decisions with a minimum of supervision.	+3	+2	+1	0	-1	-2	-3
18.	Safety and security are important to me.	+3	+2	+1	0	-1	-2	-3
19.	Having good resources and tools with which to work is important to me.	+3	+2	+1	0	-1	-2	-3

Scoring:

Transfer the numbers you circled to the appropriate place in the chart below.

Statement No.	Score	Statement No.	Score
9	___	2	___
10	___	3	___
12	___	18	___
17	___		___
Total	___	Total	___

Self-Actualization Needs   **Safety/Security Needs**

Statement No.	Score	Statement No.	Score
6	___	1	___
8	___	4	___
13	___	15	___
16	___	19	___
Total:	___	Total:	___

Ego/Esteem Needs   **Basic/Physiological Needs**

Statement No.   Score

Record your total scores in the chart below by marking an "X" under the number of your total score for that area of needs motivation. Once you

5	_____
7	_____
11	_____
14	_____
Total:	_____

have completed this chart, you can see how strongly you are motivated by these needs. There is, of course, no "right" answer. What is right for you is what matches your actual needs. This is specific for each situation and each individual.

Social/Belonging Needs

-12 -10 -8 -6 -4 -2 0 +2 +4 +6 +8 +10 +12

Self-Actualization

Ego/Esteem

Social/Belonging

Safety/Security

Basic/Physiological

SELF-ACTUALIZATION NEEDS: creativity, self-expression, self-fulfillment, use of potential, independence, feeling of usefulness, productivity, achievement

EGO or ESTEEM NEEDS: sense of self-worth, self-respect, self-identity, dignity, importance, privacy, respect from others, status, recognition, freedom, excellence, power.

SOCIAL or BELONGING NEEDS: acceptance, equality, affiliation, affection, tolerance, intimacy, support, productive relationship(s) with others, companionship, team spirit.

SAFETY and SECURITY NEEDS: comfort, preparation for the future, self-preservation, protection, safe environment, justice, stability, freedom from threat or injury.

BASIC or PHYSIOLOGICAL NEEDS: food, oxygen, water, sleep, sex, elimination, activity, normal body temperature, shelter.

Circle the specific needs that are most important to you.

Based on Abraham Maslow's "Hierarchy of Needs"

THE PARENT, ADULT, AND CHILD IN YOU

The PARENT records all imposed, unquestioned, external events that are perceived and experienced through the five senses by a person between birth (some say even before birth) and roughly age five (**taught** concept of life). Everything the child saw his parents do and heard them say is recorded in the PARENT. Freud called this the SUPEREGO.

The ADULT records information gathered and processed through exploration and testing (**thought** concept of life). Freud called this the EGO.

The CHILD records inner events (feelings) in response to external events (mostly from mother and father) between or before birth and roughly age five (**felt** concept of life). All of the responses of the child to what he or she sees and hears, the "seeing, hearing, feeling, and understanding" body of information, is stored in the CHILD. Freud called this the ID.

The ADULT begins gradually to emerge around ten months. Adult information accumulates as the child becomes able to find out for himself or herself the differences between the "taught concept of life" in his or her PARENT and the "felt concept of life" in his or her CHILD. The ADULT develops a "thought concept" of life based on the gathering and processing of information.

The ADULT is primarily concerned with transforming events, both internal and external, into bits of information and processing and filing that information on the basis of previous experience.

One important function of the ADULT is to examine the information in the PARENT to see if it is still true and if it still applies today and, then, to accept or reject it. Likewise, it examines the CHILD to see if the feelings there are still appropriate to the present time or if they are no longer valid.

The goal is not to do away with the PARENT and CHILD but to be free to examine those bodies of information and reevaluate their meaning to the present moment in which one is living. A secure youngster is one who finds that most PARENT information is reliable. Insecurity develops from having to find meaning and understanding from one's own experience and learning because of inadequate PARENT information. Maturity comes as one successfully develops a healthy and balanced ADULT self-concept.

--Based on Tom Harris, "I'm OK, You're OK."

TRUTHS THAT WILL SET YOU FREE

1. To err is human. Romans 3:21-23; 1 John 1:8
2. You can't please all people all of the time. Colossians 3:23 & 24; Galatians 1:10
3. Problems usually get worse when avoided. Philippians 3:13 & 14
4. It isn't what happens to you that makes you unhappy, it's how you look at it. So, even when things don't go your way, you can still be happy (content) with the proper attitude. Acts 20:22-24; Philippians 4:11-13; James 1:2 & 3
5. Our feelings, whether pleasant or unpleasant, are caused by how we think. Proverbs 23:7

6. No one really has it all. Everyone has gaps in his or her life. 1 John 2:15-17; 1 Timothy 6:7-10
7. Your worth is tied to who you are, not to what you do. Galatians 3:10 & 11
8. Life is rough. A great deal of hardship and frustration is built into it. John 16:33
9. Life is sometimes fair and sometimes unfair. Ecclesiastes 8:14
10. Patience is a virtue. It is often healthier to delay gratification than to seek immediate gratification. Galatians 6:7 & 8; Proverbs 14:29
11. People have both good and evil inside of them, and they seem as bent on self-destruction as they seem on growth. Jeremiah 17:9; Matthew 15:19; Romans 3:10-12; Galatians 5:19
12. It takes two to tango. Marriage problems are rarely one person's fault. Romans 2:1
13. Hard work in marriage is the norm, not the exception. It means that you and your partner need each other's help to work out personality flaws and weaknesses. 1 Corinthians 7:28b
14. No one person can meet all of your needs. Your needs can best be met through a variety of sources. Philippians 4:19
15. Your spouse doesn't really "owe" you anything for what you do. You do what you do out of love or because, at some level, you choose to do it to fill some need. You aren't owed anything for what you choose to do. 1 Peter 5:5b
16. Marriage requires change. People who refuse to change stagnate themselves and their marriages. The important issue is deciding what we need to change about ourselves and what we don't. Hebrews 12:14a
17. Every person is unique and can't be a carbon copy of anyone else. God is not a Xerox machine. It would be boring if it weren't that way. 1 Corinthians 12:18 & 19
18. We are not the target or cause of everything that happens to us. Many things that happen to us are not meant personally and are more a statement about the person who did them than about us.
19. While some issues in life are black/white, many issues are some shade of gray. Black/white issues need to be seen as black or white, but issues that are gray need to be seen that way.
20. What happens to us in the present is not necessarily what has to happen again to us in the future. History doesn't have to repeat itself.
21. Feelings aren't facts; feelings are feelings and can often cloud our judgment or deceive us.
22. Romans 5:8; Ephesians 2:8 & 9
23. John 8:11; Romans 5:8

SEVEN FOUNDATIONS OF A HEALTHY SELF-IMAGE IN CHRIST

1. **God Loves Me** - God so loved me that he gave his only Son so that, if I believe in him, I may not perish but may have eternal life. God did not send his Son into the world to condemn me but that I might be saved through him (John 3:16 & 17). God proves his love for me in that, while I was still a sinner, Christ died for me (Romans 5:8).

2. **God Forgives Me** - If I confess my sins, he who is faithful and just will forgive my sins and cleanse me from all unrighteousness (1 John 1:9).

3. **I Belong To God** - When I received and accepted him, he gave me power to become a child of

God (John 1:12). Led by the Spirit of God, I am a child of God. If I am his child, I am an heir, an heir of God and joint heir with Christ. If I suffer with him, I may also be glorified with him (Romans 8:14, 17).

4. **I Am Worth Something To God** - God created me in his image; in the image of God he created me (Genesis 1:27). It was God who formed my inward parts; he knit me together in my mother's womb. I praise him, for I am fearfully and wonderfully made. Wonderful are his works; that I know full well. My frame was not hidden from him, when I was being made in secret, intricately woven in the depths of the earth (Psalm 139:13-15a).

5. **God Has A Purpose For Me** - By grace, I have been saved through faith, and this is not my own doing; it is the gift of God, not the result of works, so that I may not boast. I am what he has made me, created in Christ Jesus for good works which God prepared beforehand to be my way of life (Ephesians 2:8-10).

6. **My Confidence Is In God Through Christ** - I can do all things through him who strengthens me (Philippians 4:13).

7. **God Is My Security** - I know that all things work together for my good because I love God and am called according to his purpose. If God is for me, who can be against me? Who will bring any charge against me, God's elect? It is God who justifies. Who is to condemn? It is Christ Jesus who died, yes, who was raised, who is at the right hand of God, who indeed intercedes for me. Who will separate me from the love of Christ? Will hardship, or distress, or persecution, or famine, or nakedness, or peril, or sword? No, in all these things I am more than a conqueror through him who loved me. I am convinced that neither death, nor life, nor angels, nor rulers, nor things present, nor things to come, nor powers, nor heights, nor depth, nor anything else in all creation, will be able to separate me from the love of God in Christ Jesus, my Lord (Romans 8:28, 31b, 33-39).

Adapted from PICKING UP THE PIECES, by Clyde Colvin Besson

I AM WHAT I VALUE, or
"Where your treasure is, there also will your heart be."

LORD, I AM OFTEN SO BUSY. THERE ARE SO MANY *IMPORTANT* THINGS I HAVE TO DO. OR, SO IT SEEMS. BUT, YOU HAVE SAID: "Seek first the kingdom of God and his righteousness, and all these things will be given you besides." (Matthew 6:33) LORD, MAYBE MY LIFE IS OUT OF ORDER. MAYBE THAT'S WHY IT'S NOT WORKING VERY WELL. HELP ME TO PUT IT BACK IN ORDER -- YOUR DIVINE ORDER.

LORD, UP TO NOW THE MOST IMPORTANT THINGS AND/OR PEOPLE IN MY LIFE HAVE BEEN e.g. God, my own way, money, education, my job, pleasure, possessions, my wife/husband, etc. (Rank order the way they *have been* up to this moment)

1. _____   6. _____

2. _____   7. _____

3._____   8._____
4._____   9._____
5._____   10._____

LORD, I *NOW* WANT THE MOST IMPORTANT THINGS AND/OR PEOPLE IN MY LIFE TO BE e.g. God, myself, my family, my children, etc. (Rank order)

1._____   6._____
2._____   7._____
3._____   8._____
4._____   9._____
5._____   10._____

THANK YOU, LORD

BEING HONEST WITH GOD, MYSELF AND OTHERS

LORD, I FIND IT EASY TO BE HONEST WITH *_____ because **
_____
_____
_____
_____
_____

LORD, I FIND IT VERY DIFFICULT TO BE HONEST WITH *_____

because ** _____
_____
_____
_____

* e.g. my mother, father, wife, husband, God, myself, friend, etc.

** complete this statement as often as necessary.

THANK YOU, LORD

MOTIVATION AND SATISFACTION

Motivation energizes and directs behavior toward a particular goal. People differ in such things as achievement, affiliation, and power motives.

A person with a strong *achievement* motive is likely to prefer challenging tasks and the opportunity to learn and master new skills.

Someone with a strong *affiliation* motive is likely to have a strong desire to be part of a team.

Someone with a strong *power* motive is likely to seek the recognition, status, and control that come from climbing the corporate ladder.

Motivation is also affected by the ways in which individuals think about and make choices and decisions regarding situations (Froman, 1986). For example, people are likely to seek a balanced or fair relationship between what they invest (education, skills, experience, time, and effort) and the rewards they receive for that investment (money, promotion, recognition, job satisfaction). People often compare themselves to others when making judgments about the equality or fairness of the relationship between what they put in and what they get out of what they are doing.

Expectancies also have a significant affect on motivation. People will be motivated to invest in activities if they expect to receive a reward for that value (Porter & Lawler, 1968).

With this in mind

- Provide clear and attainable performance standards
- To the extent possible, rewards for hard work and outstanding performance should take a form that is important to you
- Be aware of the clear relationship between obtaining those valued rewards and achieving a high level of performance.

Finally, goals affect motivation. Goals help direct attention, focus efforts, increase persistence, and foster action plans (Locke et al., 1981). You are more likely to motivate yourself if you set goals that are specific, attainable, and moderately difficult. However, these goals should not be set in concrete. They should be flexible enough to accommodate new developments.

GOAL-SETTING WITH THE LORD

LORD GOD, I DON'T ALWAYS KNOW WHERE I AM GOING OR HOW TO GET THERE. BUT, YOU DO. YOU HAVE A PERFECT PLAN FOR MY LIFE THAT INCLUDES EVERYTHING I WANT THAT IS GOOD FOR ME. I NEED YOU TO HELP ME SORT THINGS OUT.

LORD, I WANT TO BE e.g. at peace, loving, joyful, etc.

1._____ 2._____ 3._____

4._____ 5._____ 6._____

7._____ 8._____ 9._____

10._____ 11._____ 12._____

LORD, I <u>DON'T</u> WANT TO BE e.g. lonely, spiteful, jealous, afraid, etc.

1._____ 2._____ 3._____

4._____ 5._____ 6._____

7._____ 8._____ 9._____

10._____ 11._____ 12._____

When you have listed all the things you want to be and don't want to be, say to the Lord first, "WITH YOUR HELP AND BY THE POWER OF THE HOLY SPIRIT, I CAN BE WHAT I WANT TO BE". Then say to the Lord, "IN YOUR STRENGTH, I DON'T HAVE TO BE WHAT I DON'T WANT TO BE. YOU HAVE SET ME FREE BY SHEDDING YOUR PRECIOUS BLOOD FOR ME ON THE CROSS AND BY FILLING ME WITH YOUR HOLY SPIRIT".

Periodically, go over the list and see how often you can substitute "I AM" for "I WANT TO BE". This will provide you a way to evaluate your growth and progress in your walk in the Spirit.

THANK YOU, LORD

GOAL-SETTING - POTENTIAL HUSBAND/FATHER

LONG RANGE GOALS:

What type of work and family situation do you hope to have?

Do you want your wife to have to work *and* be a wife/mother?

What are your plans for work or career?

MEDIUM RANGE GOALS:

What are your education and training plans?

What is the next step in your career?

SHORT RANGE GOALS:

What are your plans for the next six months?

What are your plans for the next year?

YOUR BOARD OF DIRECTORS

1. Write the names of the five most important and/or influential people in your life. Leave space for #2.

2. Next to each name list the following:

    a. A value or idea which he or she has taught you

    b. One significant detail about his or her background.

    c. The setting that you visualize when you think of him or her.

    d. A quote that you associate with him or her.

THIS IS THE BOARD OF DIRECTORS OF YOUR LIFE.

Examine your Board of Directors. What does it say about you? What does it say about your values? What does it say about what is important to you?

Think about your Board of Directors. Decide which one has been or presently is the most influential to you. Write his or her name below. Why is this one the most influential

Read the following

TOWARD A HEALTHY SEXUALITY

For centuries, the prevailing theological teaching attributed no more than a functional character to human sexuality. Corresponding to the sexuality of the animal world, it was evaluated chiefly or entirely on the point of view of procreation.

On the basis of an anthropology, or study of man, that is concerned with the totality of the person, new points of view for the understanding and evaluation of sexuality present themselves nowadays, leading to changes of emphasis and additional insights, and making the current teaching more complete.

Sexuality must be numbered among the essential determining factors of the human being, whether as man or woman, and affects the behavior of the individual, even in his or her mental attitudes and processes.

Statements in Revelation

The statements of the Old Testament have preserved humankind's primal consciousness of one's own human nature and one's created existence as man or woman. This sexual differentiation has been determined by the Creator and expresses part of what is contained in the assertion that humans are made in the image of God (Genesis 1:27).

The entire person is created good. Therefore, sexuality as a gift from God is entirely good. The relationship of man and woman united in love reflects something of God's love, in its free giving of itself, and of the unity within the Divine Trinity. Man and woman are to help complete each other through communication with the person who is the partner of the opposite sex. The goal of each is to do everything possible to help the other reach Heaven, one's ultimate goal.

The similarity of sound in the Hebrew terms *ish* (man) and *isha* (woman) could be seen as already pointing to the fact that in this "partnership" there is fundamentally no subordination and superiority. The "two-in-one-flesh" connotes more than a passing sexual relationship of man and woman. It expresses the total unity which both form, breaking through even the bonds of blood and family (Genesis 2:22-24)

The total surrender in the sexual act is termed in the Old Testament "knowing". In this profound interpersonal meeting, both parties reveal themselves in their deepest personal sphere of intimacy; irreversible knowledge and self-revelation come about. Beyond this, human beings receive from God in principle the responsibility of the transmission of life (Genesis 1:28).

The New Testament takes up a natural attitude to sexuality and nowhere connects it with the ritual laws of purification of the Old Testament. Jesus replaces it with a fundamentally new concept of purity -- right intentions come from the heart (Mark 7:1-23). Through the proclamation of the kingdom of God now beginning in Jesus, however, the future and final condition of human beings is emphasized to such an extent that sexuality and its fulfillment in marriage no longer appears as the only normal or universal way for human beings in this world.

The way of virginity, or consecrated single-hood, appears beside it as a genuine possibility (Luke 20:27-36). Also, in the relationship to Christ, the difference of the sexes becomes a matter of indifference, of like value (Galatians 3:26-28).

Anthropological Analysis

The sexual difference between man and woman constitutes an essential part of human nature. It finds expression in the psychological make-up of the person and may not, therefore, be regarded in isolation or in a merely functional way. Everybody lives in the sexual situation, male or female.

Sexuality is not something added on to a neutral human nature but determines the person as man or as woman. For the development of human personality, sexuality is of considerable significance. Long before marriage, one comes into the field of force of one's sexuality and is molded by it. How one's body image is developed and the presence or absence of adequate role models have an important influence in this area. Thus, sexuality must be dealt with not only in relation to marriage but also has a place in all anthropology.

Only in the differentiation between man and woman can the human potentialities and roles be realized to the full. In sexuality, the person experiences one's insufficiency and dependence on the "You" of the other, and that, first of all, on the human plane, on the partner of the opposite sex.

Inasmuch, however, as sexuality, even when finding its realization and fulfillment in marriage, is still lacking an ultimate fulfillment, it points beyond to something outside of the human life-partner. A person achieves the deepest fulfillment only in the meeting of the "You" of God. This Christian understanding of the person as one "called" by God and with a "calling" to fulfillment with God makes possible for the Christian a deeper view and evaluation of human factors and permits him or her to come to a certain understanding of the transcendental relationship of the person through the lack of entire fulfillment in human sexuality.

The actual primary sexual relationships, if they are to correspond to the nature and dignity of the person, must always be contained in the framework of *eros*, in the affection and love that is directed to the entire person of the other and accepts the other not merely for the sake of one's own need but also loves him or her as a person. But, this acceptance will correspond fully to the dignity of the other person only if it takes place nor merely ego-centrically in a self-gratifying self-love but is joined to a love that gives itself, is prepared to make sacrifices, and is directed to the "You" of the other, a love that is ultimately a weak reflection of that love of God for humans that entirely offers and gives itself.

Where sex and *eros* become separated from the personal, and sexual activity is no longer the means and expression of personal attachment but sought for its own sake, it loses its natural meaning and legitimacy. This is what happens with pornography, pedophilia and ephebophilia, incest, homosexual activity, and all other forms of sexual abuse, with gratuitous recreational sex that uses the other merely as an object for self-gratification, even if mutually sought, with the impersonal use of sex in advertising, and with the casual portrayal of the sexual act outside of a meaningful context, such as is evidenced in modern books, TV, movies, and plays. Sexuality stands entirely at the service of the personal and must not be separated from it.

Total sexual self-giving leads to the giving and receiving of a knowledge and completion that affects the entire person. Where such knowledge and completion take place, those involved cannot part as though nothing has happened. But, neither can they enter the total life in common that makes it possible unless the irrevocable will to share their entire life is present, is expressed in a binding way, and is accepted by both sides. Thus, the indispensable prerequisite for the legitimacy of the sexual act is the mutual and publicly proclaimed will to a binding acceptance that is total and permanent. Only in validly contracted monogamy is the full meaning of such a self-giving secured.

When sex breaks away from the totality of human love, in the attempt to be autonomous and a law unto itself, the person experiences "the effects of sin," the dissolution of the inner harmony. Where sex is separated from the personal, it begins a vagabond life. There appears, then, no reason why the "partner" should not be changed at will. All promiscuity, whether homosexual or heterosexual, indeed all sexual chaos is a sign of a personal crisis on the part of the one concerned.

Formation of Sexuality: Sublimation

The enormous excess of energy contained in the sexual drive and the plasticity of human sexuality indicate that a person has the capacity of putting these powers at the service of further human purposes, of sublimating them. This redirection does not imply a repression of the sexual impulse but, rather, a positive reapplication of them for other spheres of fulfillment in life.

Sigmund Freud describes sublimation as a change in the goal as well as in the object of the drive so that what "was originally a sexual drive finds a fulfillment that is no longer sexual but has a social or higher ethical value." Freud sees sublimation as the de-sexualization and also the socialization of this drive. Precisely the freely chosen and inwardly accepted sacrifice of the actualization of sexuality, when it represents a genuine acceptance and re-formation of these drives, permits the release of great energies of mind and body that can express themselves in significant achievements of a charitable, religious, or cultural nature.

Sublimation is, therefore, the reorganization of sexual drives into a more widely inclusive human attitude. It presents itself for everyone as a task and is a prerequisite for the maturing of personality as also for the success of all interpersonal communication. Where no genuine formation of this drive takes place, but only a repression, the road to personal maturity remains blocked. This can lead ultimately to false attitudes, reactive over-compensations, or perversions.

Consequences for Moral Behavior

The right evaluation of sexuality demands, first of all, a firm acceptance of one's own sexuality and its development as well as a knowledge of the power and inner dynamics of sex and *eros*, of the dangers of false repressions, and of the place of true sublimation of these powers. Hence, the encounter with the partner of the opposite sex cannot be treated casually.

In correct companionship, which is also incumbent on the unmarried, important forces in both man and woman are released that help toward an integration of the entire sexual faculty and preserve from dangerous repressions without, however, leading to inappropriate sexual activity. Since all sexual relationships connote a mutual personal self-revelation and a certain surrender, they should take place only in full knowledge of this responsibility, that is, in remote or proximate preparation for marriage.

The right attitude toward sexuality forbids both all prudery and also all pornographic and gratuitous exhibitionism; it calls for an acceptance of the sense of modesty. Stress should be laid especially on the total human implication of modesty, namely to protect the intimate personal sphere from unjustified intrusion. Yet, the limits of what is included in detail under modesty cannot be determined merely on Christian or religious grounds. It depends very considerably as well on the particular cultural tradition and on what precisely is likely to endanger the intimate sphere of the person.

Pope St. John Paul II has written, "sexual modesty cannot, then, in any simple way be identified with the use of clothing nor shamelessness with the absence of clothing and total or partial nakedness. There are circumstances in which nakedness is not immodest. Nakedness as such is not to be equated with physical shamelessness. Immodesty is present only when nakedness plays a negative role with regard to the value of the person, when its aim is to arouse sexual desire, as a result of which the person is put in the position of an object for enjoyment. The human body is not in itself shameful for the same reason as are sensual reactions and human sexuality in general. Shamelessness (just like shame and modesty) is a function of the interior of a person." - *"Love and Responsibility"* 1981.

Thus, nakedness cannot be condemned in principle. This is evidenced by the fact that nudity has always been accepted and venerated in art, even by the Church. A naked body is simply a naked body, the viewing of which, even in a family context, does not in itself lead to inappropriate sexual behavior among siblings. In fact, a casual acceptance of nakedness as nothing to be ashamed of can lead in children, with proper parental teaching and guidance, to a psychologically and spiritually healthy body image and understanding of one's own and another's body as an integral part of the total person, created as good by the Creator and, thus, to be given due respect, honor, and dignity. In this way, parents can enhance the development of a healthy sexuality in their children.

Sexuality possesses for personal human development and for integration into human sexuality such a decisive significance that its theoretical or practical rejection in principle entails a serious disorder. Such rejection is to be reckoned as an objectively serious offense against the structure of human existence and action. With regard to the question of guilt, one must also take into consideration the modern knowledge coming from depth psychology. The judgment of individual failures may not be made without taking into consideration the total basic attitude and intention of the person concerned.

Both repression of natural desire for pleasure as well as a self-centered, autoerotic acceptance of sex are to be rejected as false forms of behavior. The same is true of pre-marital sexual intercourse: it could create a disturbance in the psychic balance of the future husband and wife. Pre-marital continence will, therefore, retain an importance that is not to be underestimated for the maturing of personality and preparation for marriage. A change in the attitude of the Church so as to favor pre-marital intercourse is not to be expected; this would essentially mar the concept of marriage. The step to promiscuity would then be a minor one. Because of the eminently super-individual significance, not only the Church but also all cultures to varying degrees have been concerned to set up some norms for sexual behavior.

--Johannes Gruendel, edited by Patrick J. Hession

SEXUAL FULFILLMENT

Individuals who have good sexual relationships with their partners are often aware of some basic facts about human sexuality.

Sexual Attitudes and Behaviors Are Learned

Your sexual attitudes have been learned. Your parents and peers have had a major impact on your sexual attitudes, but there have been other influences as well: school, Church, and the media. Your attitudes about sex would have been different if the influences you were exposed to had been different.

The same is true of sexual behavior. The words you say, the sequence of events in lovemaking, the specific behaviors you engage in, and the positions you adopt during sexual intercourse are a product of your culture and the learning history you and your partner have had.

The fact that learning accounts for most sexual attitudes and behaviors is important because negative patterns can be unlearned and positive patterns can be learned.

"The secret of a good sexual relationship is making love *with* your partner, not *to* your partner." Dianna and Kenneth Lowe, Married Couple

Time and Effort Are Needed for Effective Sexual Communication

"Psychosexual health is strongly related to a woman's communication with her partner about sexual needs." Ferroni & Talle (1997). Talking about sex may seem awkward. Overcoming awkward feelings requires retraining yourself so that sex becomes as easy for you to talk about as the latest movie.

Spectatoring Interferes with Sexual Functioning

Spectatoring involves mentally observing in an evaluative way your sexual performance and that of your partner. Spectatoring interferes with each partner's sexual enjoyment because it creates anxiety about performance, and anxiety blocks performance. The desirable alternative is to relax, focus on and enjoy your own pleasure, and permit yourself to be sexually responsive.

Physical and Mental Health Affect Sexual Performance

Effective sexual functioning requires good physical and mental health. Regular exercise is related to higher libido, sexual desire, and intimacy (Ash, 1986). Low self-esteem, which may lead to depression, may also influence your sexual desire and performance.

Good health also implies being aware that some drugs may interfere with sexual performance. Too much alcohol can slow the physiological processes and deaden the senses. The result of an excessive intake of alcohol for women is a reduced chance of orgasm; for men, overindulgence results in a reduced chance of attaining an erection.

Anti-depressants may also depress sexual functioning. For example, Paxil and Prozac may delay ejaculation in men and interfere with orgasm in women.

Self-Knowledge and Self-Esteem

Sexual fulfillment involves knowledge about yourself and your body. Such information not only makes it easier for you to experience pleasure but also allows you to give accurate information to your partner about pleasing you. It is not possible to teach a partner what you don't know about yourself.

Sexual fulfillment also implies having a positive self-concept. If you do not like yourself or your body, you might wonder why anyone else would.

A Good Relationship

Your sexual relationship is part of the larger relationship between the partners. What happens outside the bedroom in your day-to-day interaction has a tremendous influence on what happened inside the bedroom.

A couple's sexual relationship positively influences the couple's overall relationship in several ways: (1) as a shared pleasure, it is a positively reinforcing event; (2) by facilitating intimacy, since many couples feel closer and share their feelings before and after a sexual experience; and (3) by reducing tension generated by the stresses of everyday living and couple interaction (McCarthy, 1982)

Open Sexual Communication

Sexually fulfilled partners are comfortable expressing what they enjoy and do not enjoy in the sexual experience. Unless both partners communicate their needs, preferences, and expectations to each other, neither is ever sure what the other wants. What you like may not be the same as what your partner wants.

Sexually fulfilled partners take the guesswork out of their relationship by communicating preferences and giving feedback. This means using what some therapists call the touch-and-ask rule. Each touch and caress may include the question, "How does that feel?" It is, then, the partner's responsibility to give feedback. If the caress or touch does not feel good, the partner can say what does feel good. Guiding and moving the partner's hand or body are also ways of giving feedback.

The following are examples of what women want men to know about women:

- It does not impress women to hear about other women in the man's past.
- If men knew what it is like to be pregnant, they would be more sensitive and understanding.

- Most women want more caressing, gentleness, kissing, and talking *before* and *after* intercourse.
- Sometimes the woman wants sex, even if the man doesn't. Sometimes she wants to be aggressive without being made to feel that she shouldn't be.
- Intercourse can be enjoyable without orgasm.
- Men should be interested in fulfilling their partner's sexual needs.
- Most women prefer to have sex in a monogamous love relationship, not before or outside of marriage.
- When a woman says no, she means it. Women do not want men to expect sex every time they are alone with their partner.
- Many women enjoy sex in the morning, not just at night.
- Sex is *not* everything. A good relationship *is*.
- Women need to be lubricated before penetration.
- Men should know more about menstruation.
- Many women are no more inhibited about sex than men.
- Women do not like men to roll over, go to sleep, or leave right after orgasm.
- Intercourse is more of a love relationship than a sex act for many women.
- Women tend to like a loving, gentle, patient, tender, and understanding partner. Rough sexual play can hurt and be a turnoff.

The following are things men wish women knew about men and sex:

- Men do not always want to be the dominant partner; women should be aggressive sometimes.
- Men want women to enjoy sex totally and not be inhibited.
- Men enjoy tender and passionate kissing.
- Women need to know men's erogenous zones.
- Many men enjoy a lot of romantic foreplay and slow, aggressive sex.
- Men cannot keep up intercourse forever. Most men tire more easily than women.
- Looks are not everything.
- Women should know how to enjoy sex in different ways and different positions.
- Women should not expect men to get a second erection right away.
- Many men enjoy sex in the morning.
- Pulling the hair on a man's body can hurt.
- Many men enjoy sex in a caring, loving, exclusive relationship.
- It is frustrating to stop sex play once it has started.
- Women should know that not all men are out to have intercourse with them. Some men like to talk and become friends.

These respective comments by men and women about the other sex emphasize the importance of being direct with your partner about sexual desires and preferences. Open sexual communication is vital to a sexually fulfilling relationship.

Sexual interaction communicates how the partners are feeling and acts as a barometer for the relationship. Each partner brings to a sexual encounter, sometimes unconsciously, a motive (pleasure, reconciliation, procreation, duty), a psychological state (love, hostility, boredom, excitement), and a physical state (tense, exhausted, relaxed, turned on). The combination of these factors will change from one encounter to another.

The verbal and nonverbal communication preceding, during, and after sexual interaction also may act as a barometer for the relationship.

David Knox and Caroline Schact, *MARRIAGE AND THE FAMILY*, 1999

Behaviors, that is, what we say and do, are an expression of attitudes we hold. Attitudes themselves are formed by ideas and events that we have experienced throughout our lives, as we have seen. One set of attitudes that affect the relationship we have with our mate, or potential mate, relate to what is often called "body image." This refers not only to how we perceive and like or dislike our own bodies but also to how we perceive and like or dislike the bodies of the opposite sex..

Attitudes and behaviors in relation to nakedness and nudity are a reflection of the ideas and events that have shaped you and will be reflected in marital behavior. This has practical application, especially when it comes to love making and sexual intercourse. Do you perceive your mate or potential mate as a "sex object" to be used for your own gratification or as a co-partner with you in the creation and propagation of new life? Are you uncomfortable having intercourse with the lights on or do you have to have them off? Even how you express simple affection, such as holding and kissing in front of your children or others, is a reflection of your attitude toward yourself and your mate or potential mate.

Pope St. John Paul II said, "Sexual modesty cannot in any simple way be identified with the use of clothing, nor shamelessness with the absence of clothing and total or partial nakedness. There are circumstances in which nakedness is not immodest...Nakedness as such is not to be equated with physical shamelessness. Immodesty is present only when nakedness plays a negative role with regard to the value of the person...The human body is not in itself shameful nor, for the same reasons, are sensual reactions and human sexuality in general. Shamelessness, just like shame and modesty, is a function of the interior of a person" *Love and Responsibility*, 1981.

COHABITATION OR "RENT-A-SPOUSE"

Cohabitation is defined as two unrelated adults who are involved in an emotional and sexual relationship and who sleep together in the same residence on a regular basis. There are over 3 million cohabitating couples in the United States. Cohabitation has been increasing at a rate of about 15% a year for the past decade or so. The following discusses cohabitation from a purely psychological and sociological perspective, but it validates the objections to this practice as a serious moral disorder because it is basically a self-centered and self-serving relationship.

Reasons offered for cohabitation include the following: fear of marriage; career or educational commitments; increased tolerance from society, parents, and peers; improved birth control technology; and the desire for a stable and sexual relationship without legal ties. Cohabitants also regard living together as a vaccination against divorce which, as we shall see, is an illusion.

Other reasons given are:

- Greater sense of well-being.
- Delaying the age at which a person marries.
- Living with an intimate partner provides an opportunity for individuals to learn more about themselves and their partners and also provides an opportunity to screen out a partner with whom marriage might not work.
- A person's values, habits, reactions, behavior patterns, and relationship expectations are sometimes more fully revealed in a living-together relationship context than in a traditional dating context. However, the same thing not only will happen but also needs to happen in an honest and open dating relationship if it is serious.
- Since living together relationships usually involve fewer legal ties, it may be easier to disengage from such a relationship than from a marriage. However, discord is more likely to lead to the termination of a cohabitating relationship than of a marital relationship.

Here are the negative consequences of cohabitation:

- Because cohabitation is often an ambiguous relationship, with partners attributing different meanings to the experience, the potential for feeling tricked or deceived is higher than in a marriage relationship, which usually has more clearly defined expectations.
- When levels of commitment are uneven in a relationship, the partner who is more committed feels used. In a one-sided convenience relationship, one partner manipulates the other to fulfill sexual, domestic, or other needs while withholding any semblance of commitment. There is little reciprocity, and the relationship become exploitive.
- Some cohabitating couples must contend with parents who disapprove of or do not fully accept their living arrangement. Some parents express their disapproval of their child's cohabitating by cutting off communication with as well as economic support for their child. Other parents display lack of acceptance of cohabitation in more subtle ways, such as excluding the couple from family activities.
- Some economic liabilities exist for those who live together instead of getting married. People who live together typically do not benefit from their partner's health insurance, Social Security, or retirement benefits. Only spouses qualify for such payments.
- For males in particular, the negative part of having a live-in partner is the loss of personal freedom (Lynch & Richards, Family Life Researchers).
- Cohabitation has been shown to attract a different type of couple than marriage and to foster attitudes that contribute to divorce (Steven Nock, Sociologist). Cohabitants are not ready to commit to each other. Cohabitants may have developed "bad habits with respect to the development and maintenance of a relationship, and these problems get imported into subsequent relationships" (Stets, 1993), e.g. a greater tendency to withdraw from a relationship and separate than to negotiate disagreements. When those who had lived together prior to marriage were compared with those who had not, the former revealed lower marital quality, higher marital conflict, and more marital problems (Rogers & Amato, 1997). The proportion of separating and divorcing within 10 years is a third higher among those who lived together before marriage than among those who did not

- (Bumpass & Sweet, 1989); DeMaris & Veninadha Rao, 1992; Balakrishan & colleagues, 1987).
- Other researchers have found lower commitment to the institution of marriage, a belief that marriage is not a lifetime commitment, and a greater perceived likelihood of divorce among couples who had cohabitated (Thomson & Colella, 1992; Stets, 1993). Cohabitants were characterized by lower-quality relationships because cohabitation is an incomplete institution. Non-marital unions are not yet governed by strong consensual norms or formal laws. What is the legitimate role of a parent in his or her offspring's cohabitating union? What is the non-marital equivalent of an in-law? What is the legal status of children born from non-marital unions? Who has custody rights when they separate?
- Cohabitants tend to be people who are willing to violate social norms and live together before marriage. Once they marry, they may be more willing to break another social norm and divorce if they are unhappy than unhappily married persons who tend to conform to social norms and have no history of unconventional behavior.
- The bulk of the available data suggests that people should not live with a partner before marriage if their sole goal in doing so is to help ensure a durable marriage with that partner.
- In one study, 65% of abused partners were in live-in situations; 19% were in traditional marriages.

--Edited by Patrick J. Hession

CONSIDER THE MOTHER OF JESUS

One of the phenomena of our century has been the Women's Liberation Movement. The result has been a mixed blessing. There have been many positive aspects as new opportunities have opened up for women. There have developed a healthier respect for and appreciation of women as equal partners with men. However, there has also been a cancerous growth of radical feminism that seeks to drive wedges of hostility, mistrust, and competition between men and women. Both the positive and the negative aspects have affected men and women alike both in the Church and in society. In sorting out the voices around us, it is important to seek the answer to the questions "What are women being liberated *from*?" and "What are women being liberated *for*?"

God did not create men and women to be in competition but to complement each other. In Genesis, we read, "God said, 'Now we will make humans, and they will be like us.' So God created humans to be like himself; he made men and women. God gave them his blessing and said, 'Have a lot of children! Fill the earth with people and bring it under your control. Rule over the fish in the ocean, the birds in the sky, and every animal on the earth.'" (Genesis 1:26-28)

All of the attributes of God exist completely in man and in woman. Some attributes God chose to express primarily in man and some he chose to express predominantly in woman. When they become "one flesh," man and woman become more than each can become separately. Their offspring receive the attributes from both the mother and the father that they need to be a complete person. The sex role identity problems that people are having today are a direct result of the confusion among their parents as to their proper role and identity under God. Men and women alike need to recapture the divine vision for them if we are to cut through the rhetoric and false philosophies of the so-called "Women's Movement".

Men need to see the Godly attributes that reside in women who would become, or who are, their wives and mothers of their children. Women need to see the Godly attributes in the men with whom they seek to unite, or with whom they are united, as husband and father of their children. Children need to see the Godly attributes of their parents if they are going to learn how to grow "in wisdom and age and favor before God and men" (Luke 2:52) as Jesus did. Only then will human beings be able to regain the dominion over the world that God gave them in the beginning. As the climax of God's creative activity, human beings resemble God primarily because of the dominion that God gave them over the rest of creation.

One woman most embodies the womanly attributes of God. I would ask you to consider the mother of Jesus. She can teach both men and women how to fully express their sexuality.

No gospel writer more fully expresses Jesus' concern for woman than Luke. For this reason, we read much about the mother of Jesus in his account.

In the first chapter of his Gospel, he tells us of the appearance of Gabriel to Mary. Here we learn that Mary was a maiden, a virgin, probably nearing or in her early teens. She wasn't sleeping around with the young guys of her day, as many junior high girls are today. She was pure, and the Lord was with her.

She was engaged to Joseph, the last stage before becoming his wife, but she hadn't engaged in premarital sex with him. Thus, she could honestly respond to the prospect of conception with the question, "How can this happen? I am not married?" (Luke 1:34)

Mary knew her position and was comfortable with it. She was a handmaid, a servant, submissive to the will of God in her life, even if she didn't fully understand it. She wasn't constantly questioning God but "kept all these things in her heart." (Luke 2:51) Her response, from which she never wavered throughout her life, even when her son was killed, was "I am the Lord's servant! Let it happen as you have said." (Luke 1:38)

She was a woman of unwavering faith. Her faith was expressed in her obedience to the Law and in her relationship with Joseph. She consecrated Jesus, the firstborn son, to the Lord as it was written in the Law of the Lord. Though they were poor, they offered the required sacrifice of a pair of turtledoves or two young pigeons, in accordance with the dictate in the Law of the Lord. (Luke 2:22-24)

Mary and Joseph practiced their religion together faithfully, and under their influence Jesus "became wise and grew strong. God was pleased with him, and so were the people." (Luke 2:52) Jesus was obedient to them.

Mary supported Jesus in his ministry and evidently accompanied him as she is often mentioned among the women who ministered to his needs. We know from John's gospel that she gently interceded on behalf of the couple at the marriage feast of Cana (John 2:3-5). She didn't make an issue of it or take over and manipulate the circumstances; she simply stated the situation and allowed Jesus to respond as he chose. Her response to the servants is her response to us, "Do whatever Jesus tells you to do."

The mother of Jesus was there when it counted. She was at the foot of the cross, when all of his followers had run away in fear. She was willing to follow Jesus, even to the cross, regardless of the possible consequences to her own life.

Finally, she was a committed member of the early community. She is mentioned among those in the upper room who devoted themselves with one accord in prayer. (Acts 1:14) Thus, she was there on the Day of Pentecost when they were filled with the holy Spirit and began to speak in different tongues as the Spirit enabled them to proclaim. (Acts 2:1-4)

Contrast this woman and mother with the "liberated" women and girls of today. Mary knew what she was liberated from - the same sin and death that you and I have been liberated from. More importantly, she knew what she had been liberated for - to be the woman, the mother, and the companion of the Son of God made man. In this, she fulfilled the womanly role for which God had created her and exhibited the Godly attributes that God had instilled in her.

This is the role model that women and girls need to see today if they are to be truly liberated. No man in his right mind could resist such a woman. No man in his right mind could abuse, or take advantage of, or divorce such a woman.

May God again raise up a generation of women of whom it may be said, "You are truly blessed! The Lord is with you." (Luke 1:28)

CHAPTER II

GOD'S ORDER FOR THE FAMILY

When an artist creates a work of art, it is intended to be an expression and reflection of the thoughts, intentions, ideas, and even personality of the artist. Thus, from the work of art, we are able to know quite a bit about the artist. When the artist, on the other hand, comes personally and explains what his or her intentions and purposes were when the work of art was created, we are able to know even more about the artist.

God has done this both in the Old Testament and in the New Testament. God's Word, the Scripture, is the written revelation of God himself made complete in his Son, Jesus Christ. God, the artist, came to explain the purpose and the intention of his creation, and we can know more about his nature and personality than would have been possible just from observing his artwork.

When God created the world, he expressed order, purpose, and variety as his aspects. (1) He showed creation to be not haphazard and accidental but purposeful and under the control of an Intelligent Being.

When God created man, he saw that it was not good for him to be alone. So he gave him a suitable helper and mate, woman, (2) and told them to multiply and become family. (3) In their unique creation, they revealed personality, the ability to create, and interrelationship as additional aspects of God.

In creation, God revealed order: material creation was to help and serve the human beings who were over it but who themselves were to be under God who created them. In the family, God was to be over the man, the man was to be over the woman, they both were to be over the children, and they all were to be over the rest of creation. (4) They were given the very authority and dominion of God over all creation (5) and were commissioned to reveal and to be an extension of God as Family.

The man was to reflect all the attributes of God the Father: the ability to beget, to rule over, and to provide for. Man, his wife, and their children were to bear a family resemblance to their Father, God. (6) They were to do this, however, in total obedience and submission to God. (7) Thus:

>GOD - Entirely superior is nature and position to man and all creation.
>>MAN (ADAM) - Dominant in position, equal in nature and super-nature to woman. Adam (man) was created first.
>>WOMAN (FROM ADAM) - Subordinate in position under man, equal in nature and super-nature to man. Helpmate to Adam (man).
>>>CHILDREN - Subordinate in position under father and mother, equal in nature and super-nature to mother and father.
>>>>CREATION - Thoughts, desires, and other things (The World). Under dominion of humans.

When the man submitted himself to the woman under him (8), instead of to God over him, he disrupted God's order. He did not exercise his proper authority under God over her when he accepted her suggestion. This was his additional act of disobedience to God's order. She did not submit her decision to her husband before she disobeyed.

Sin, therefore, came from two areas: 1) the woman's disobedience to God and man's submission to her and to her act of disobedience, and 2) their failure to exercise their positions as God had established them. Family, then, became a reflection of man's disorder instead of God's order. With disorder in the family came disorder in the world. Thus:

> CREATION - Thoughts, desires, and things (The World). Exercise control over humans.
> > CHILDREN - Rebellious, disobedient to parents, self-centered..
> > > WOMAN - Unsubmitted, "liberated" in wrong sense, self-centered, afraid to discipline children.
> > > MAN - Unsubmitted to God, domineering, self-centered, afraid to discipline wife and children.
> > > > GOD - Irrelevant, not considered in decision-making, ignored.

So, it still is today. Neither the world nor the Church can be any stronger than the families that make it up. The critical need today is the restoration of God's order within the family. To do that, we must see and understand God as Family.

When Noah built the ark, he did it according to the pattern that God gave him. (9) When Moses built the tabernacle and the Ark of the Covenant, he was ordered to do it according to the pattern that God showed him. (10) The pattern for the family that God has given us is the Trinity: God the Father, God the Son, and God the holy Spirit - separate and distinct Persons but one intimate and indissoluble unity. The family is intended to be the primary reflection of the order that exists within the Godhead.

That order consists of an interrelationship of authority, mutual submission, and love between and among interdependent Persons. It is the proper functioning of this order between man and woman in the world that makes marriage and, when children are begotten, family. That is why God hates divorce. It is a destruction of the intimate and indissoluble unity of husband and wife that is to be reflected in marriage and, then, in the family.

God called Abraham and continued the process of revealing the basic nature and life of the Godhead as Family. The promise to Abraham, that he was to be the father of many nations and that his descendants would be as numerous as the sands of the seashore and the stars of the heavens (11), was an expression of the will and purpose of God the Father himself - to beget many spiritual children. God's own desire was to enlarge his family by sharing his life with human beings.

As in the beginning, the family of God was to be the fruit of obedience to and trust in the authority of the Father. Once more, God revealed himself as Father, and his children were to be a people called by his name, identified as begotten by him, and bearing his resemblance. The family was to reflect the intimate nature and relationship of God as Family. Through family,

God would once again restore human beings to full authority and dominion over creation.

When God called his children out of Egypt, he began to reveal two other aspects of his Fatherhood - his position as ruler and provider. Through Moses, God established for himself *his* rightful authority over human rulers. Through his people, he began to restore *their* rightful authority under him over all creatures and nations. The family of God as a whole, as well as in the individual members, was to reflect the rulership of God over all creation. But, it was through the individual families, clans, and tribes that God would extend and build up his own family.

Through the fire (12), the cloud (13), the water from the rock (14), the quail (15), and the manna (16), God revealed himself as a Father who provides for all human needs. Never once in their wandering in the desert did any of God's family lack food and provision (17). Even their shoes and clothing did not wear out during their years of wandering (18).

The whole Old Testament, more than anything else, is the story of God the Father's attempt to restore his family by bringing his children into obedience to his rulership and trust in his provision so that they could reflect his nature as Family. Through obedience and submission to the Law, which reflected the authority and love of the Father, the man could once more reflect the order within the Godhead and regain his position as ruler over and provider for his own family.

At its best, however, the human family was only a poor reflection of what God desired. It was, and is, only in and through Jesus Christ that the full revelation of God as Family came. God revealed himself as Father, and the Godhead as Family, when he said, "This is my beloved Son with whom I am well pleased; listen to him" (19). Because Jesus is revealed as Son, we know God fully as Father. He it is who shows us the Father for he said, "Whoever has seen me has seen the Father" (20). He alone bore the true resemblance to his Father by his total obedience and submission even to his death on a cross (21).

He is the Son, under the authority of the Father, who does only what he sees the Father doing (22) and says only what he hears the Father saying (23).

He is the Son, who shows us that it is only through submission and obedience that a man can exercise true authority over his own family and within the family of God, the Church.

He is the Son, who tells us that, before our family can reflect the true order of his Family, we must be begotten from above, that is, by his Father (24). For we are born of our parents unto disorder. We must be born again of God and become his sons and daughters if we are to become true fathers and mothers (25).

Being married in a church doesn't make our marriage and family Christian or Godly. We must individually accept Jesus Christ as our Savior and the Lord of our own personal life and then of our marriage and family. Making him the central third-party to our marriage unites our family with his Family through the holy Spirit. In this way, our family becomes the highest reflection and extension of the Trinity, and God can accomplish his plan and purpose through our family on the earth. In this kind of family, in turn, our children can discover and develop their true identity as persons called and gifted by the Father, saved and restored by the Son, and empowered and sent forth by the Holy Spirit to accomplish the will of the Father for them.

So it is that God the Father continues in our day to extend his Family on the earth. Humanity's most desperate cry today is for real family. Our deepest, innermost search is for the Father because only a true father can provide the strength, leadership, and provision that gives us security. We must become the father and the family that God desires and intends for us to be!

The world cannot be any better than the families that make it up. The Church will never be any stronger than the families under Christ within it. Satan knows this and is putting forth every effort as never before to destroy the family.

Witness the high divorce rate.

Witness the absence of fathers and the number of families trying to be held together by mothers who are not uniquely equipped by God to be fathers also.

Witness what is happening to our children as a result. Homosexuality and lesbianism are not an accident but the result of the inability of a child to discover and to develop its true identity without a true father model. Both the male and the female need the father *and* the mother to develop a healthy, integrated personality.

Witness the destruction of potential family members through abortion. God the Father never delegated the right and authority to do this to a woman, her parents, her husband if she has one, her doctor, our lawmakers, or the court!

Nor for that matter did God the Father delegate the right and authority to couples to prevent conception through artificial means of birth control. He did give couples the right to make decisions with him about family size and to use natural means such as Natural Family Planning to bring this about. However God is the *sole* author of life! The same attitude that claims the right to *prevent* birth artificially is the same one that claims the right to *terminate* it through abortion. We are to cooperate with him but we have *no* right or authority to block his ability to create life through us by means of artificial devices, pills, or creams.

Yes, the most critical need today is the restoration of God's order within the family! God's purpose in the Garden of Eden, thwarted by man's and woman's disobedience, is to be the goal of God's restoration of all things in Christ, the obedient Son. As Head of the Christian marriage, he restores order to the family. Through our obedience to him, he teaches us love for and submission to the Father. However we must also let the Holy Spirit of unity-in-love seal our marriage and our family as never before. If God's order is not reflected in our family, to that extent it will never be reflected in the world or in the Church.

The Trinity is a Family in order! The family founded on God reflects the authority, submission, and love between and among interdependent persons that exist within the Trinity. This is God's will for us, his people. As we accept his will, we become in our day the reflection and extension of the Family who is God. In our truly Christian family, we discover and develop our true identity in Christ as his brothers and sisters and as sons and daughters of his Father. Can there be a higher calling?

(1) Genesis 1:1-2:4
(2) Genesis 2:18, 21-24
(3) Genesis 2:27 & 28
(4) Genesis 3:16
(5) Genesis 1:26, 28; See also Psalm 8
(6) Genesis 1:27
(7) Genesis 3:2 & 3
(8) Genesis 3:17
(9) Genesis 6:14-16
(10) Exodus 25:8 & 9
(11) Genesis 17:4-8, 22:17 & 18
(12) Exodus 13:21
(13) Exodus 12:22; Numbers 9:15-23
(14) Exodus 17:6; Numbers 20:8, 11
(15) Numbers 11:31 & 32
(16) Exodus 16:3-18
(17) Exodus 16:35; Deuteronomy 29:5 & 6
(18) Deuteronomy 29:5
(19) Matthew 17:5
(20) John 14:9b
(21) Philippians 2:6-11
(22) John 5:19 & 20, 30, 36b
(23) John 8:28; 13:49 & 50
(24) John 3:3,5
(25) John 3:6 & 7

PRINCIPLES FOR MAKING NEW FRIENDS AND FINDING A POTENTIAL MATE

One area for which too many people fail to prepare adequately is the selection of a potential life-mate. Much is left to chance or infatuation. On the other hand, many feel a strong pressure to date even if they are not ready or choose not to date. There is no negative Scriptural stigma attached to choosing not to date, in the sense of an exclusive relationship with one person, until you are ready to establish a permanent and stable relationship. You must see choosing not to date at all as a personal choice and preference. In reality, you are called by God to be single until or unless he calls you into marriage.

More and more people choose to remain single or to postpone marriage until later in life. You may prefer to live alone for a substantial period of your life. You may discover many satisfactions in living alone and may not see this lifestyle as a temporary arrangement. You may choose to dedicate your single lifestyle to a deeper commitment in Christian service to others. It is important that, whatever your choice, you resist efforts by well-meaning relatives or friends to get you to give up the single lifestyle until you choose to do so. It is important also not to compromise by becoming involved in immoral sexual relationships in the name of satisfying a perceived need for intimacy. There is a very important difference between being lonely and being alone. The deepest and most important personal gift you can give to your potential life-mate is your self, complete, unused, and undefiled.

The following are some principles for making new friends of both sexes and for finding a potential mate when you are ready.

- Take part in activities that you do well, that you enjoy, and that allow you to be your natural self without trying to impress someone of the opposite sex.

- Become involved only in an environment in which others who share your values and ideas would most likely gather. Examples would be church groups or volunteer, community, and political organizations.

- Become involved in your work or other activities because you see them as valuable in themselves. People are naturally attracted to a busy, serious-minded person.

- Social occasions such as parties or picnics are natural places to meet friends of both sexes. Stay involved in group social activities until you are sure that you are ready to become involved in an exclusive relationship.

- Before you date, determine the qualities and qualifications that you are looking for in a potential mate. Be sure to look for someone whom you will be able to respect and trust.

- Don't date beneath yourself. That is, don't lower your standards and values that you have determined to look for in a potential life-mate. You will only devalue your own self-respect.

RESPONSIBILITIES TOWARD ONE ANOTHER

Wisdom should be the foundation of your life and marriage. "By wisdom a house is built, and by understanding it is established; by knowledge the rooms are filled with all precious and pleasant riches." (1) Wisdom is the ability to apply knowledge to practical, real life situations. If you lack wisdom, you should ask God who gives to all generously and ungrudgingly, and he will give it to you. (2).

"The beginning of strife is like letting out water so stop before the quarrel begins." (3) This doesn't mean that you should never discuss anything. Nor does it mean that you should never express your strong *feelings* about your convictions or always give in. It does mean that you need to stop senseless arguments about things that really aren't that important or over which you have no control. A senseless argument, like a forest fire, very quickly gets out of control.

The foundation of any human relationship is *mutual respect*. If you lose respect for each other, you will quickly fall into infidelity in speech, if not in action. "Let marriage be held in honor by all, and let the marriage bed be kept undefiled. God will judge fornicators and adulterers." (4) Husband, you should love your wife as you love yourself, and wife, you should respect your husband " (5)

"The husband should give to his wife her marriage rights, and likewise the wife her husband. The wife does not have authority over her own body, but the husband does. Likewise, the husband does not have authority over his own body, but the wife does. Do not deprive one another except perhaps by agreement for a set time to devote yourselves to prayer. Then, come together again so that Satan may not tempt you because of your lack of self-control." (6) Your sexual relationship must be an expression of your *love* not of your *lust*. There are times to refrain for the sake of your spouse, but don't make your sexual relationship a weapon against your spouse. Make it a true expression of mutual intimacy to be enjoyed by both, not endured by one.

(1)	Proverbs 24:3		(4)	Hebrews 13:4
(2)	James 1:5		(5)	Ephesians 5:33
(3)	Proverbs 17:14		(6)	1 Corinthians 7:3-5

SOME IMPORTANT QUESTIONS TO HELP YOU PREPARE FOR MARRIAGE

What is the most important thing you should consider when thinking about the right person to marry?

It is wise for you to screen your choice of a mate with your head before you "fall in love" with your heart. Once your heart is involved, your head doesn't have much of a chance.

In trying to predict the kind of mate someone will make, a careful look needs to be taken at the family from which the man or woman comes. The only thing more important than the family in mate selection is the person's faith.

Provided that his or her parents have a reasonably healthy marriage, you would be wise to marry into a family much like your own. Even if the parents are not happily married, the less social distance a couple attempts to span in their own marriage, the safer from social stress their marriage will be.

If one marries into a family that is too different from his or her own family, everyone is uncomfortable. Although God values each member of both families, the social distance between the families creates painful discomfort for the couple and puts unnecessary stress on the marriage. Simply stated, couples from similar families are more likely to be compatible in marriage than couples from families who are very different from each other.

Can you expect to change your spouse into an ideal mate regardless of family background?

Basically, marriage doesn't change people that much. What a person is in his or her family, he or she is most likely to be in marriage. You see people like they really are when you see them in their families. To go into marriage believing you can change things about your mate that you strongly dislike is to be tragically naive.

What is the recommended length of courtship?

Somewhere between six months and two years is about right.

In what ways are the marriages of today's youth different from those of their parents?

The roles of husband and father/wife and mother are much more flexible today than they were in the past. Today, the Church and Society accept either a traditional marriage or a companionship marriage.

In the traditional marriage, only the man works outside the home. The woman works inside the home, devotes herself to homemaking as a career, and assumes major responsibility for raising the children. The man provides for the family, maintains the home, and disciplines the older children.

In a companionship marriage, both spouses work outside the home. Parental responsibility, house management tasks, and business decisions are shared.

You will need to talk about which of these models you and your potential mate want for your marriage early in the courtship process. If major conflicts are obvious, it is wiser to seek someone else whose views of marriage are more like your own.

Don't economic forces seem to direct which type of marriage to choose?

Every couple has to determine whether its standard of living will dictate the model of marriage, or whether the model of marriage will determine the standard of living the two can afford.

Every couple deserves the freedom to make this decision itself. You cannot make a career woman happy by making her feel that her place is in the home. It only frustrates her and makes her angry. If God has given her gifts that she believes cannot be satisfactorily expressed in the home, she needs the freedom to be a good stewardess of those gifts.

So, you should be very open in discussing your futures and needs with each other. If a woman needs and wants to work outside the home, she will need to marry a man who wants a companionship marriage. If a man wants and needs a traditional marriage, then he should marry a woman whose gifts are fulfilled in homemaking.

In what ways are the attitudes of children from single-parent families different from those who live with both of their parents, especially when it comes to their expectations of marriage?

Most single-parent families can't adequately prepare young people for life. Gender role identity and marital role expectations are two examples of vital areas in which children from single-parent families suffer deficits in facing their future.

There is a correlation between the erosion of the two-parent family and the increase of homosexuality in our society. Most youngsters need continuing healthy interaction with both of their parents in order to achieve a wholesome sexual identity.

A father plays an extremely important role in the gender identity of his child. The father furnishes the male child with his model of masculinity. A girl's femininity is also rooted deeply in her relationship with her father. More feminine mothers do not raise more feminine daughters.

When the father is absent from the home during the child-rearing years, the children's efforts toward obtaining healthy identities are adversely affected.

Children raised in single-parent families are also deprived of an opportunity to observe successful marriage role models in their parents. Some people raised in single-parent families determine to learn from their parents' mistakes what they couldn't learn from their examples. However, these people are exceptional. Most children raised in single-parent families face much higher risks of marital failure than do youngsters from healthy two-parent families.

What is the primary difference between Christian and non-Christian marriages?

Christian marriage is more than a contract. It is a covenant entered into by two people before God and under the Lordship of Jesus Christ. So, when there are times in Christian marriages when couples are unhappy, their commitment to Christ holds them in their marriage. This allows the Holy Spirit to use the dispositions of Christian mates to help the spouses toward spiritual and emotional maturity.

Adapted from an interview with Dr. Richard Dobbins in *CHARISMA*, March, 1986. Dr. Dobbins is a pastor/psychologist who specializes in Christian marriage and family life. He is the founder of Emerge Ministries, Inc., in Akron, Ohio

CHRISTIAN PRINCIPLES FOR HELPING YOU TO A STRONG, ENDURING MARRIAGE

1. You need to become more and more conscious of what your behavior is saying about marriage. What message do others get from your behavior when you are around them? Do you compliment others, especially women? Are there obvious glances or hugs of affection? Is your love for others obvious to them? Are you jealous? Review the evaluations you did earlier in regard to your own behavior to help you better prepare for marriage.

2. You and your potential mate need to know that Christian marriage is for life. Therefore, as a Christian, you will need to select your potential spouse very prayerfully and carefully. You must not see divorce as an option for you.

Christian spouses, *both of whom profess to be living in obedience to God's Word*, cannot divorce. They must seek sound marital counseling to work out their problems. If they choose to divorce, they do so in direct disobedience to the Scriptures. This act of disobedience may not affect their ultimate salvation, but it does carry with it a certain tragic harvest.

3. You need to be learning what the Scripture teaches about the conduct of a Christian man toward his wife and a Christian woman toward her husband. This will give you valuable help in determining to what extent your behavior conforms to what the Scripture says about Christian marriage.

4. Christian married love is a persistent effort on the part of two people to create for each other the circumstances in which each can become the person God intended each other to be, a better person than each could become alone.

--adapted from an article by Dr. Richard Dobbins, pastor/psychologist and founder of Emerge Ministries, Inc., Akron, Ohio

ENHANCING YOUR CHANCES FOR AN ENDURING AND HAPPY MARRIAGE

More than half of marriages today result in divorce. Many other couples are less than satisfied with each other. How can you enhance your chances of a marriage as God intended it, one that stays alive, vibrant, and well? In addition to the other ways discussed so far, the following are some suggestions that can help you:

1. **Maintain a Positive Attitude toward Each Other**. The reason most often given for an enduring and happy marriage is a generally positive attitude toward each other. "Misery loves company" but is not an ingredient for a happy marriage, Christian or otherwise. Your chances for happiness are greater if you see your mate as your best friend and like him or her as a person. Look again for those qualities in your spouse that drew you to him or her in the first place. They haven't gone away!

2. **Strive for Passion, Intimacy, and Commitment**. True love is an *action*, not a *feeling*. Passion or feeling is the quickest to develop and the quickest to fade. If that is all you have, your relationship will be in trouble. Although passion peaks in the early phases of a relationship, it still matters to the long term success of the marriage.

Intimacy is a feeling of emotional closeness. It develops slowly but becomes more important as a successful relationship matures. Both persons find it increasingly important to understand and to meet each other's wants and needs, to listen to and to support each other, and to share values. One requirement for intimacy is that each of you has established your own identity as a person.

Commitment develops the most slowly but is the factor that holds the relationship together, especially during the difficult times which are a part of any relationship. Without passion and intimacy, however, commitment tends to be shallow.

3. **Maintain Separate Identities**. A non-possessive and healthy relationship is one in which both of you maintain separate identities and strive for personal fulfillment. "Becoming two in one flesh" does not mean that you swallow each other up but that your two identities, joined together, become stronger than either one could ever be separately.

In a non-possessive relationship, each person can pursue different interests of his or her own choosing. However, if you pursue non-possessive relationships too far, you can begin to drift away from each other. You must find the right balance between maintaining separate identities and spending enough time together to remain close.

4. **Communicate Regularly**. Good and frequent communication is vital for creating and maintaining a loving relationship. Communication is the *glue* that holds people and relationships together. It is helpful to have periodic communication sessions in which you share with each other almost anything that is on your mind. Topics can be both positive and negative. An important aspect of this process is that you share both facts (what happened) and feelings (how you feel about what happened).

5. **Maintain Open and Honest Communication**. Honest communication is essential for any

good relationship. However, it is important to be wise and sensitive in your openness. When what you say allows the other person some alternatives, openness is more acceptable. It also helps to express your feelings in a constructive rather than a destructive way. Keep the focus on how *you* feel rather than judging or blaming the other person. Also, describe what your spouse is saying or doing (behaviors) rather than character traits.

The **DESC Script** can be a helpful tool, especially when strong emotions arise in your conversation.

Describe what your spouse is saying or doing that is causing a problem for you.

Express the effect this is having on you and how it makes you feel.

Suggest something else that your spouse can say or do that won't cause a problem for you.

Consequences – Tell your spouse what will probably happen if he or she does what you suggest in improving your relationship.

6. **Keep Your Relationship Alive**. Unfortunately, many relationships drift into a rut or routine. Try pleasant surprises to keep your marriage relationship fun and vibrant.

CONFLICT AREAS THAT OFTEN NEED
TO BE SETTLED IN MARRIAGE

Housing: A major source of satisfaction or dissatisfaction in life is your basic living accommodation. Having a place to come home to in which you can take pride can be a source of comfort. On the other hand, coming home to a place that you consider a source of stress can contribute to a feeling of depression. We all need a certain amount of comfortable "space" so crowding can contribute to a feeling of stress also. Perhaps, with children, the house will become too "small" or the neighborhood too congested. Therefore, you will need to give your housing a high priority in your budget.

People define "adequate living" in vastly different ways. Your definition will also vary at different times in your life as we have just seen. You will need to evaluate what kind of housing you want or need and where.

Will you want to live in an apartment, house, or mobile home? Will you want to live in the country, city, or small town? What kind of housing will you be able to afford? In considering this, the cost should be based on the husband's income *only* in most cases, even if both of you will be working. This is to keep housing from becoming a source of stress if children come along or the wife loses or decides to quit her job for any reason.

Conflicts: Conflicts are a normal part of life and are neither positive nor negative in themselves. They arise frequently in both work and personal life. *How* you resolve conflicts determines to a great extent whether they have positive or negative outcomes. It is important to resolve conflicts quickly and before they fester and develop into a more destructive form. Some conflicts may be very difficult to resolve by yourselves, so you may need to consider mediation as a voluntary method. Mediation services are increasing around the country and can be found through your Yellow Pages.

The most common and destructive conflicts occur between people who are emotionally involved with each other such as spouses and family members. Statistics indicate that you are more likely to be killed or injured by a spouse or family member than by a stranger.

Common areas of conflict within marriage are triggered by infidelity, table manners, TV preferences, visitation of or by in-laws, holiday visitations, responsibility for household tasks, money, and friends. You should talk over these and other areas of potential conflict with your potential spouse.

The following are some ground rules for resolving marital conflicts:

1. **Maintain good two-way communication**. Intelligent communication, as we have seen, is the *glue* that holds people and relationships together. It is a God-given and uniquely human ability but one of the most difficult to develop. You will need to work at it constantly.

2. **Restate what you think you heard your potential mate say.** Many conflicts intensify because those involved never stop to really *listen carefully* to what the other person is trying to say. If you are not sure whether you heard what he or she said correctly, try to restate it as you

heard it. This gives him or her the opportunity to correct or to clarify the communication. Then, express your *feelings* about the matter communicated.

3. **Define the *real* problem**. Often, what you or your potential mate grumble about is not the real issue in the conflict. Try to get to the *need* that he or she believes is not being met and find ways to meet that need. Refer to the needs list at the beginning of this workbook.

4. **Stick to the issue.** When strong feelings start arising in a conflict, they often tend to get out of control and cloud the real issue. There is, then, a natural tendency to bring old wounds and past hurts into the conflict. Stick to the issue at hand. Old wounds and hurts can and should be dealt with later.

5. **Don't hit below the belt.** This refers to something that is unfair such as things that you did in the past that have been corrected or forgiven by God. If you want to live together in harmony after the conflict, don't dig up the past or open old wounds.

6. **Be ready and willing to compromise.** Most issues have more than one side so compromise is usually possible. You should be willing to meet the other person half-way. Be aware, however, that there are some principles that you cannot compromise so be honest about them.

7. **Avoid manipulative pressure.** A common way to manipulate is to promise a little favor or reward in return for getting your own way. Most people can see through manipulation and end up feeling resentful toward you, especially if techniques you use involve withholding love or approval.

8. **Be willing to go the extra mile.** To keep the relationship a live and vibrant one, there are times when one side will have to make a major concession to the other. Be willing to sacrifice something you want, but don't need, for the sake of the other. Things will balance out in the long run.

Work or Career: Situations in which you or your potential spouse will have jobs or careers of some psychological or economic importance are increasingly common. Two critical factors that influence this situation are the rising aspirations of women and the high cost of living. If you want a marriage where both persons continue to work or develop a career, you will need to discuss and to resolve the following factors:

1. **Feelings of competitiveness.** These can often exist, even with both persons have a modern outlook. What if the wife gets a promotion instead of the husband? What if she makes more money than he does?

2. **Sharing decisions equally.** Major decisions require the collaboration of both husband and wife. Such a decision could be relocating to another town or city. What if the wife's company wants to transfer her and the husband has to quit his job to go with her? Other decisions involve investing money, buying or building a house, and starting or increasing a family. Any decision that involves major long-term consequences needs to be thoroughly discussed and all *feelings* regarding it need to be expressed honestly and openly. Otherwise, they will become areas of frustration or resentment later.

3. **Dividing household chores equitably.** Many women who work outside of the home rightfully complain that they are responsible for too much housework. This can lead to major conflicts between spouses. One suggestion would be to divide the household tasks in some equitable manner such as according to preference or the amount of effort involved.

4. **Share being inconvenienced**. Certain tasks are considered inconvenient because they have to be done during regular working hours. Take turns being inconvenienced by taking the time off to accomplish these tasks. An example may be picking up a sick child at school or taking a child to the dentist.

5. **Plan and develop adequate support systems for child care.** It is a real challenge to balance adequately work and child demands. One way to do so is to develop a diverse support system. Simply arrange with at least three people, including relatives if possible, who are willing to help you out in an emergency.

6. **Plan for both of you to be active parents**. A dual career family with one or more children can only function smoothly when both parents take an active interest in child rearing. Both parents must regard spending extensive time with each or all of the children as their *primary* responsibility under God. In fact, the healthy psychological and spiritual development of the child or children *requires* that they do so. When both parents work, taking a child to the doctor is as important for the father as it is for the mother.

7. **Decide how finances from dual incomes are to be handled.** The major area of conflict in most marriages is finances. This can be especially complicated when there is income from a dual career. Many couples find that the additional expenses, such as a second car and its related expenses, actually prevent them from getting ahead financially. Unless carefully managed, two incomes in one family can cause special problems. Should some money be allocated from each income for common expenses? Should all the income be put into a common fund for all expenses, including allowances? Should there be one joint checking account and two personal checking accounts?

UNDERSTANDING YOUR POTENTIAL MATE

In trying to understand the kind of person your potential mate is, it will be helpful to take a look at the family from which he or she comes. As we have seen, the reason is that we have been formed to a significant extent, for good or for bad, by our parents. We say and do what we do because that is the way we were taught.

Dr. Richard Dobbins, a pastor and psychologist who specializes in Christian marriage and family life, states the following: "Marriage generally does not change people that much. What a person was in his or her family, he or she is most likely to be in marriage. To believe that you can change things about your mate that you strongly dislike is to be tragically naive." However, if you understand some of the family influences and how hard it is to change things in yourself, it will be easier to understand and to accept your potential mate the way he or she is.

The following evaluation should be done together with your potential mate. It can open up areas for understanding and communication that can strengthen your marriage relationship and lead to significant psychological and spiritual growth and healing.

POTENTIAL WIFE'S FAMILY EVALUATION

1. What does her mother (step-mother) think about men? _____

   _____

2. How are (were) boys and men treated in her family? _____

   _____

3. Does (did) her mother (step-mother) compliment her father (step-father)?   YES ( )   NO ( )   NOT VERY OFTEN ( )   OFTEN ( )

4. Is (was) her mother (step-mother) affectionate with him?   YES ( )   NO ( )   NOT VERY OFTEN ( )   OFTEN ( )

5. Does (did) here mother (step-mother) still seem to be in love with her father (step-father)?   YES ( )   NO ( )   SHE DOESN'T SHOW IT ( )

6. Does (did) her mother (step-mother) still make herself attractive to her husband?   YES ( )   NO ( )

7. Does (did) her mother (step-mother) admire and respect her husband?   YES ( )   NO ( )   IT IS HARD TO TELL FROM HER ACTIONS ( )

8. Does (did) she respect his leadership?   YES ( )   NO ( )

9. Does (did) she yield when he makes or made major family decisions?   YES ( )   NO ( )   COMPLAININGLY ( )

10. What kind of housekeeper is (was) she?   NEAT ( )   MESSY ( )

11. Is (was) she involved with her children?   YES ( ) NO ( )   With your potential wife specifically?   YES ( )   NO ( )

12. How well has she cared for her children?   VERY WELL ( )   MODERATELY WELL ( )   AS WELL AS SHE WAS ABLE ( )   POORLY ( )

13. Is (was) she ambitious?   YES ( )   NO ( )   EXCESSIVELY ( )

14. Can (could) she cook?   YES ( )   NO ( )   SOMEWHAT ( )   WELL ( )

15. Does (did) she continue to develop her mind?   YES ( )   NO ( )

16. Is (was) she a reader?   YES ( )   NO ( )   SOMETIMES ( )

17. Does (did) she abuse alcohol or other drugs, including prescription drugs?   YES ( )   NO ( )

18. Does (did) she abuse your potential wife physically?   YES ( )   NO ( )   verbally?   YES ( )   NO ( )   sexually?   YES ( )   NO ( )

19. Is your potential wife close to her mother (step-mother) in a healthy way?   YES ( )   NO ( )   MODERATELY ( )

20. Is your potential wife close to her father (step-father) in a healthy way?   YES ( )   NO ( )   MODERATELY ( )

21. Is her relationship with her mother (step-mother) happy?   YES ( )   NO ( )   MODERATELY ( )

22. Is her relationship with her father (step-father) happy?   YES ( )   NO ( )   MODERATELY ( )

23. Is your potential wife's mother (step-mother) a committed Christian?   YES ( )   NO ( )

24. Has your potential wife forgiven her parents for anything they may have done to or against her, whether intentional or not?   YES ( )   NO ( )

Adapted from an interview with Dr. Richard Dobbins in CHARISMA, March, 1986

Read the following

OTHER IMPORTANT ACTIVITIES TO COMPLETE

1. Think of one personality trait that characterizes you (e.g. honest, polite, adventurous, funny, etc). Give examples of how others have contributed to that aspect of your self-concept. What have others said or done that has contributed to your developing that aspect of your self-concept?

2. Think of an example of someone such as parents or schoolmates conveying a negative image of you during your childhood. Describe how such negative labeling affected you. How did it make you feel about yourself? Does it still affect your self-concept?

What did you learn from these activities?

3. The ego-ideal theory of love suggests that we fall in love with someone who has qualities we admire but lack in ourselves. To apply this theory to yourself, write the heading "I WOULD LIKE TO BE MORE...." on a piece of paper. Under this heading, make a list of qualities that you wish to have or improve in yourself (e.g. self-discipline, responsible with money, etc.). Then, think of the qualities of your mate or dating partner (or previous partner). Place a check mark next to each quality under your heading that describes your current or previous mate or dating partner. Place an asterisk (*) next to each quality on your list that describes your ideal partner. What did you learn from this activity?

4. Think of someone in your life that you believe you have not adequately expressed your love to. This person may be someone who had died or who is currently living. Write a letter to this person in which you fully express your love. When you finish, ask yourself what you learned from doing this activity. How did it feel to approach this activity? How did you feel after finishing it?

5. Make a list of 10 important characteristics or qualities that you want in a partner. Then, think of either a) the person you are currently involved with, b) the last person you were involved with, or c) the person you would like to be involved with. Evaluate the person according to the list of 10 important qualities you generated. How many of the qualities and characteristics does this person have? What did you learn from this activity?

6. Make a list of issues couples should address before making a marital commitment, whether discussed in this workbook or not. Be prepared to share your list with your partner or future partner.

7. Identify a married couple whom you view as happily married and who are willing to participate in an interview. The couple should be married for at least five years. Interview the couple and note their response to the following questions:

a) How long have you been married?
b) How did getting married change your relationship?
c) What characteristics or qualities do you think are important to maintain a happy marriage?
d) What specifically do you do as individuals and as a couple to maintain marital happiness?

What did you learn from this activity?

8. Identify an individual who has been a parent and interview the parent by asking the following questions:

a) In your experience, what has been the most rewarding aspect of parenthood?
b) In your experience, what has been the most difficult aspect of parenthood?
c) If you could go back in time and do anything different in your parenting, what would it be?

What did you learn from this activity?

9. Find a stepparent who is willing to participate in an interview about stepparenting. Record the stepparent's responses to the following questions:

a) How long have you been a stepparent?
b) What is the age and sex of each of your stepchildren?
c) What do your stepchildren call you?
d) What is the best part about being a stepparent?
e) What is the most challenging part about being a stepparent?
f) What advice would you give to other individuals who are in (or about to enter) the stepparenting role?

What did you learn from this activity?

10. The top money questions to ask before you get married.

What does your balance sheet look like?

A balance sheet, or net worth statement, is simply a snapshot of your financial condition that shows what you would have left if you sold all your assets and paid off all your debts.

A negative net worth might be a sign of trouble, but first take a hard look at the numbers. Did you fiancé just finish medical school with a bunch of student loans, or is it car loans and credit card debt tipping the balance into the red? It makes a difference.

What is your credit rating?

Even better than asking the question would be exchanging credit reports. You can order copies of your credit history from several Websites. Take advantage of the opportunity to check over your own credit report. Mistakes are not uncommon.

Why should you care about your partner's credit rating? Each other's debts are in your name, and unless you transfer them to a joint, you are not responsible for the other's debts. However, joint purchases such as a house will be affected by the other's credit rating. You may get stuck with less favorable terms such as higher interest rate or a smaller mortgage. The credit report will also give you some insight into how your partner manages debt.

Do you want children?

Of course, there are lots of reasons to discuss having children. You have already considered this in another exercise. However, having children is a financial decision as well. Will both of you continue to work full time? What kind of childcare would you arrange? What happens if the baby is sick and can't go to the baby sitter? Who has the more flexible schedule or is willing to adjust work hours in an emergency?

How was money handled while you were growing up?

Financial planners often ask this question as a way of gauging clients' attitudes toward money. The answers can be revealing. If money was a hushed subject you your partner's family, he or she may be uncomfortable discussing finances with you. Perhaps, money and gifts were used to show affection in your own family, and you will be deeply hurt if your new spouse doesn't continue the tradition.

Obviously, neither of you is a clone of your parents, and free-spending parents sometimes produce thrifty children, but some insight into your partner's background can help you understand his or her attitudes today.

What are your financial goals?

Discussion about dreams and goals will probably span the length of your marriage, but it is important to begin talking before you say, "I do." Start with the big picture: When would your partner like to reach financial independence? What is his or her idea of the perfect career? Would he or she ever want to branch out on his or her own? Does he or she think parents should pay for every dollar of your children's college education?

Then move on to more near-term goals: buying a house, saving for big-ticket items such as vacations and cars, developing a budget and tracking expenses.

What did you learn from this activity?

USING YOUR ENGAGEMENT PRODUCTIVELY

Engagement moves the relationship of a couple from a private to a public experience. Family and friends are invited to enjoy the happiness and commitment of the individuals to a future marriage. The engagement period is your last opportunity to systematically examine your relationship, ask each other specific questions, recognize relationship patterns, visit future in-laws, and participate in premarital counseling. All of the exercise have been designed to bring you to this point in planning for marriage if you have taken them seriously. Before you commit to an engagement, carefully and prayerfully review the following information based on solid psychological and sociological, as well as biblical, principles.

Examine Your Relationship - The Roman poet, Ovid, wrote, "Before you run in double harness, look well to the other horse."

"Pay me now or pay me later" applies to the consequences of using or not using your pre-engagement or engagement period to examine your relationship. At some point, you will take a very close look at your partner and your relationship, but will you do it now or later? Doing so now may be less costly than doing so after the wedding.

Recognize Dangerous Relationship Patterns - As you examine your relationship, you should be sensitive to patterns that suggest you may be on a collision course. Three such patterns include breaking the relationship frequently, constant arguing, and inequality resulting from such differences as education and social class. A roller-coaster engagement is predictive of a marital relationship that will follow the same pattern. The same is true of frequent arguments in relationships. However, a relationship pattern characterized by lack of communication may be just as unhealthy as a relationship pattern characterized by arguments.

Recognize Potentially Problematic Personality Characteristics - Individuals may have characteristics that should be viewed with concern. People don't change that much after marriage, and you can't change your partner very much, no matter how much you may want to or think you can. Nor can you "save" them. Only God can!

Three such personality characteristics that predispose individuals toward impaired functioning in marriage are poor impulse control, hypersensitivity to perceived criticism, and exaggerated self-appraisal.

Persons who have poor impulse control, especially anger, have little self-restraint and may be prone to aggression and violence. Lack of impulse control is also a problem in marriage because the person is less likely to consider the consequences of his or her actions.

Hypersensitivity to perceived criticism involves getting hurt easily. Any negative statement or criticism is received with a greater impact than you or another person intends. The disadvantage of such hypersensitivity is that you may learn not to give feedback for fear of hurting the hyper-sensitive partner. Such lack of feedback blocks information about what you do that upsets the other and what you could do to make things better. Hence, the hypersensitive one has no way of learning that something is wrong, and you have no way of alerting him or her. The result is a relationship in which neither of you can talk about what is wrong.

An exaggerated sense of one's self is another way of saying that the person has a big ego and always wants things to be his or her way. A person with an inflated sense of self may be less likely to consider your opinion in negotiating a conflict and may prefer to dictate an outcome. Such disrespect for you can be damaging to the relationship.

Observe Your Future In-Laws - Engagements often mean more frequent interactions with each partner's parents, so you might seize the opportunity to assess the type of family your partner was reared in and the implications for your marriage. Some of the exercises in this workbook are designed to help you do this for your own family as well as for your potential spouse's.

Keep in mind that there are at least six people in a marriage--before the kids come. These are the partners and each partner's parents and/or stepparents. A potential groom is likely to be a husband much like his father. A potential bride is likely to be a wife much like her mother. When visiting your in-laws, observe their standard of living, the way they relate to each other, and the degree to which your partner is similar to his or her same-sex parent. Observe also how your partner relates and responds to his or her parent of the opposite sex. That is most likely how he or she will relate or respond to you when you are married.

Such comparisons are significant because both you and your partner will reflect your respective home environments to some degree. If you want to know what your partner may be like in twenty years, look at his or her parents of the same sex. There is a tendency for a man to become like his father and a woman to become like her mother. Those who report positive childhood relationships with their fathers and mothers are more likely to report high-quality marriages. This is especially true for females (Holman & Olsen, 1997).

Consider Premarital Education - This workbook, of course, is a form of premarital education. However, after you are engaged, it is good to take advantage of premarital counseling in some form.

Although the Catholic Church has a mandatory requirement for marriage preparation, most clergy suggest three premarital sessions before the wedding. These sessions consist of information about marriage, an assessment of the couple's relationship, and/or resolving conflicts that have surfaced in the couple's relationship. A professional marriage counselor may also be helpful in assisting a couple to assess their relationship. Some premarital counselors use inventories to help identify couples who are likely to get divorced. Couples who have unrealistic expectations, poor communication patterns, absence of conflict resolution skills, etc. are more likely to separate than those who score high in these areas.

Give Your Engagement Period Time - Impulsive marriages where the partners know each other for less than a month are associated with a higher-than-average divorce rate. Partners who date each other for at least two years before getting married, without cohabiting or engaging in premarital sex during that time, report the highest level of marital satisfaction. A short courtship does not allow a partner to observe and scrutinize the behavior of the other in a variety of settings..

Consider Disapproval From Parents, Siblings, And Others - Parental or other predictions (whether positive or negative) often come true. If the predictions are negative, they may contribute to stress and conflict once the couple marries.

Even though parents who reject the commitment choice of their offspring are often regarded as unfair, their opinions should be taken seriously. The parents' own experience in marriage and their intimate knowledge of their offspring combine to help them assess how their child might get along with a particular mate. If the parents of either partner disapprove of the marital choice, the partners should try to evaluate these concerns objectively. Parental insight might prove valuable.

Consider Dysfunctional Relationship Dynamics - As mentioned above, communication and conflict management patterns are predictive of relationship trouble in marriage. Partners who belittle each other (even if they call it "just kidding"), hold back what they really think or feel, withdraw from an argument, and think seriously about what it would be like to be with someone else are less likely to stay together.

Are You Having Second Thoughts? - If you are having second thoughts about getting married to the person to whom you have made a commitment, you are not alone. Although some anxiety about getting married is normal because you are entering a new role, constant questions to yourself such as "Am I doing the right thing?" or thoughts such as "This doesn't feel right" are definite caution signals that suggest it might be best to call off the engagement or wedding. When in serious doubt, don't go through with the wedding!

MARRIAGE

Sociology and History of Religion

Sociologically speaking, marriage is a sexual fellowship, the structure of which varies considerably according to general social conditions. It cannot be denied that extraordinarily various forms of marriage in fact exist and that the Christian definition of marriage as a life-long, indissoluble union between one man and one woman is recognized, in this strict form, only by Christians themselves.

Monogamous marriage, however, though dissoluble in certain circumstances, is very widespread indeed and is associated with no particular form of culture. Polygamous marriage is favored by complex social conditions where there is a particular demand for female workers, or where prestige and the desire for numerous offspring is involved.

The factors that determine the concrete structure of marriage can never be sought merely in terms of sex-life and sexual hygiene, or merely in terms of the relationship between man and woman. They are above all the needs of family and society, that is, the demands of education, economics, property, social security, public morals, and the like. This is so because, in the long run, general social conditions are decisively affected by married life and family life.

So marriage has never been regarded as the private business of the two partners. It has always been fitted into the supra-individual, general human context of morality and religion and always considered to exist in view of the family, law, morals, and ethical rules which concern themselves more with this ordination than with the needs of marriage as such.

Hence, marriage, in the history of religion, is an objectively prescribed order that involves the partners in cosmic relationships. It is often held to have been instituted by the Supreme Being as a special state of life that can only be entered upon through ritual initiation. Wedding brings a new status; it is a turning point in the life of a person, like birth, puberty (admission among adults), and death, and determines whether we can speak of marriage or not.

As a rule, the marriage rite is celebrated only once between one man and one woman, although a wider range of sexual relationships of one sort or another is often permitted. In any case, the wedding makes marriages valid in the eyes of the community. There is really no personal relationship that can compare in importance with this state of marriage created by the wedding.

So we see that the idea of marriage as something willed by God is more deeply rooted in people's religious consciousness than one might at first suppose, considering the wide range of sexual relationships permitted in various cultures.

In order to gain as clear an insight as possible into marriage as the Church understands it, we must realize what a multitude of forms marriage may take and at the same time bear in mind the features common to those many forms.

Marriage in Historical Revelation

The creation narrative says that woman was created for man's sake, man being in need of help and completion. Woman is created as a suitable helper for Adam, as it were "opposite him". She is to be his lifelong companion. A man leaves father and mother for his wife's sake and becomes one flesh with her precisely because it is only in her that he finds all of himself -- only with her can he enter a union that has no parallel in the human order. It is even closer than the bond of descent with his father and mother. Humans, created male and female, are instructed to be fruitful and to fill the earth.

In the New Testament conception of marriage, another feature of the creation narrative plays an important part. It is the affirmation that the sexes are "hierarchically" ordered one to another -- that Adam's nature is the measure of Eve's nature.

This primordial priority and subordination underlies the whole relationship between the sexes, making their union possible. The priority, therefore, does not aim at favoring an individual but completion in oneness. The difference in position between man and woman is to be appreciated in terms of the oneness that is its goal and fruit. That difference gives each sex its own dignity and at the same time presupposes equality of value.

Man's dignity consists in being woman's head, woman's dignity in being the brightness and the glory of man. This priority and subordination is part of the order of creation. The judgment pronounced upon woman (Genesis 3:16) does not turn it into a moral and juridical subordination but simply recognizes a fact that, as a consequence of sin, woman will not only find many a burden in motherhood but will also be subjected to violence and exploitation at the hands of man. This is not a rule of conduct, implying that things ought to be so.

The Hebrew notion of marriage was "naturalistic," which looked with favor on marriage, children, and intercourse within the limitations set by the force of circumstances. In the New Testament, Jesus deepens the Hebrew conception of marriage in two respects.

On the one hand, he spiritualizes it, not only forbidding the dismissal of the wife as an offense against the basic law of marriage contained in the creation narrative and ingrained in human nature, which makes man and wife one flesh, but also teaching that divorce does not sever the marriage bond since he declares that the re-marriage of divorced persons is adultery. Thus, he indicates that the deepest purpose of marriage in God's eyes is the oneness of man and wife.

On the other hand, Jesus consistently states that marriage is a kind of life proper to this age, which will pass away with it. In Heaven, there will be no marrying. Compared with the kingdom of God and its demands, marriage becomes a matter of secondary importance, and the concerns of marriage must yield to the claims of his Second Coming in glory.

Jesus doubtless had this relative conception of marriage (with respect to the end) in the foreground of his mind, yet not in such a way as to lose sight of the value that marriage represents in its own right. After all, it was at a marriage feast that he performed his first miracle. Rather, that value, which God himself gave it, was set in a special light. At the same time it became clear that the value of marriage is a limited one when we consider the kingdom of God.

In St. Paul's writings, he tells us (I Corinthians 6:12-20) that sexual union is not merely a marginal erotic function but an act that, by its very nature, so absorbs and expresses the whole personality as to be an entirely unique kind of self-revelation and self-commitment. Then, he stresses the spiritual equality of man and woman and makes it clear that in Christ the differences between the sexes, with all that they entail, are relatively unimportant.

Above all, Ephesians 5:21-33 interprets Christian marriage as mirroring Christ's marriage with the Church, which in turn is foreshadowed by Adam's relationship with his wife, Adam being a type of Christ. This means that in their marriage man and wife preserve the relationship between Christ and the Church and reflect it in their relationship so that the union of man and wife not only is compared to Christ's union with the Church but also is actually based on it. Thus, when husbands love their wives as their own flesh, they are only doing what Christ does with the Church. But this great mystery of the love of Christ for the Church is mysteriously prefigured, according to Ephesians, in the text of Genesis 2:24 about the mutual relationship of the sexes, and goes to constitute Christian marriage.

Accordingly, the relationship between man and wife is theologically set apart from all other human relationships -- that, for example, between children and parents -- of which it is only said, for instance, that they should be "in the Lord." Thus, we are given a view of marriage that makes it possible and necessary to regard marriage as a sacrament in the dogmatic sense.

According to the same text of Ephesians, conduct must agree with the relationship: wives are to be subject to their husbands "in all things." This subjection, however, is to the husband who for his wife's sake must lord like Christ. Only when he is lord unto her salvation does obedience become wholly possible. So, the injunction to love one's wife is correlated with the injunction to obey one's husband.

In the Churches founded by St. Paul, women enjoyed a favored position, considering the outlook and standard prevalent at the time. He asserts their equal dignity and equal rights as had never been done before, raising marriage from the all too material state in which he found it onto a spiritual and personal plane. His letters contain the definite beginnings of a specific Christian spirituality for married people, of which too little was made later.

His pastoral wisdom and theological insight make him affirm that marriage is necessary on account of the structure of human beings, and that to avoid disadvantages married people should not abstain from intercourse except for a sound reason and a short time. Because husband and wife no longer belong to themselves, they may not refuse each other except by mutual agreement, and by Christ's command neither must leave the other. Only by the death of one of the partners is the marriage-bond dissolved. Thus, Paul not only spiritualizes the "naturalistic" Jewish view of marriage but also shows how fragile it is.

Sex and Marriage

We can say, then, that according to Genesis 2:18 and Ephesians 5:21-33, the nature of marriage is a mutual completing and perfection of the marriage partners through their union, which finds its strongest expression in sexual encounter. But, the immanent meaning of marriage points beyond itself to a transcendental purpose -- personal and physical fruitfulness arising from the union and therefore common service of the world, especially begetting and bringing up children -- the family. This purpose, intrinsic to marriage and yet transcending it, flows from the way in which man and wife are ordered to each other in marriage, and necessarily follows from the nature of their union and the sexual act, which are ordained to fruitfulness. Being married perfects man and woman not only in their manhood and womanhood but also in the oneness that is proper to marriage. That union, which embraces every dimension of the personality, has a sexual dimension and therefore includes the ordination of sex to fruitfulness.

Marriage being thus intrinsically ordered to fatherhood and motherhood, sexual love exhibits fatherly and motherly characteristics from the first, as sexual behavior shows. By giving human beings a share in God's creative power, consummated union orients the partners to the human beings it brings forth. We must not, however, conclude from the fact that marriage is ordered to the child that marriage apart from children is meaningless or even non-existent. In that case, all marriages that were known in advance to be childless, or which eventually proved to be such, would be invalid. On the other hand, marriage is ordered not only to sexual encounter but also to procreation, and that so essentially that no one may contract a valid marriage on the understanding that there will be no sexual union or no children. Even where the partners *intend* to abstain, the *right* to sex is admitted; and the exclusion of children on principle invalidates the matrimonial contract.

Mutual Completion

If marriage is seen as a saving state that leads to religious and moral perfection, then its fundamental law must be the duty of the partners to do whatever will foster the love that completes and unites them and avoid whatever will frustrate and destroy it. They must orient themselves as companions to the transcendent purpose of marriage that makes their complementing union possible -- fruitfulness not merely biological but also moral and religious thanks to their new religious situation. The final criterion of what concrete acts foster or frustrate marriage must always be what acts befit the partners as such. Completion means concretely that the husband helps the wife to be a woman, and the wife helps the husband to be a man. The partners are to affirm each other in their differences, each thus helping the other to find selfhood.

The specific completion that marriage offers is of a sexual nature and must, therefore, be sought in the realm of sex. But, it must be remembered that, while sex is directly biological, it is indirectly affected by sociological, economic, and psychological factors and, therefore, also by spiritual and religious factors. And so, completion is to be sought in all of these domains in the way appropriate to each; the same is true with selfhood. However much it unites the partners, marriage must not impose uniformity but help each toward real manhood and womanhood -- which are always intrinsically ordered to fatherhood and motherhood. Hence, the choice of a partner must be made with care, taking everything into account, from religion to eugenics, which is the study of hereditary and genetic influences. It is all the more vital to consider eugenic factors, especially in the matter of children. The balance between mutations and elimination in humans now seems to be closer to the point where any further burdening of the inheritance might well jeopardize the continued existence of humankind.

Mixed Marriages

Marriages between persons of different religions present a special problem in this respect. While inevitably on the increase, they always make the common life of the partners considerably more difficult, the more in proportion as the partners have firm convictions of the religious dimension in marriage. Marriage already has a religious character in that it embraces the total human being, including his or her moral and religious dimensions.

As a rule, one cannot simply say that differences of religion between the partners need not matter if only they are tolerant of each other, for tolerance makes co-existence possible but not oneness. By the nature of the case, the disadvantages of a mixed marriage are even plainer when the marriage is blessed with children. The child is not only the fruit of physical union; the development of his or her personality is decisively affected by the totality of the unity of his or her parents' marriage.

So it is a mistake to look on mixed marriage as an admirable field for missionary work, for the attainment of each partner's special perfection presupposes common thinking and feeling to a high degree. It will be all the more effective the more the partners have humanly in common. The same ways of thinking and acting are more a foundation of marriage than a result of it. Mixed marriages come nearest to being justified where there is no religious prejudice, a different thing from tolerance, especially where the lack of prejudice is combined with receptiveness to religion.

Faithfulness to Each Other

The union of husband and wife calls for a partnership so intimate that it is neither possible nor desirable outside of marriage. It means strict solidarity and absolute faithfulness and the closest intimacy at every level including the bodily one. This is what makes adultery so grave at its various levels.

Partnership and independence, however, do not conflict in marriage. They nourish each other because love addresses the other person in his or her freedom and tries to persuade, not to coerce, when sacrifices are necessary for the sake of the partnership. It follows that partnership ceases at the point where either partner attempts to abuse the other for selfish ends. Any such attempt, and any readiness to let oneself become the slavish instrument of the other, is sinful, the more grievously so the more personal judgment, freedom, and responsibility are violated.

Difficulties of adjustment in marriage are necessary but also may result from differences of origin or upbringing, ingrained habits, crowded living conditions, insufficient acquaintance with one another, and so on. They can be overcome only by a gradual growth in understanding and love. This is especially important when one is planning to establish a marital relationship but has not yet entered into it. All of these factors must be thoroughly addressed, discussed, and agreed upon before a permanent relationship is established.

Marriage Looks beyond Itself

Marriage must not be lived as solitude for two, for the completion and union marriage brings tends of its own nature to make the partners more open to God and to their neighbor. Moral and religious fruitfulness, when the circumstances are right, should also take concrete shape in physical fruitfulness, marriage widening out into the family. The aim must not be to produce as many children as possible but to found a family that will be qualitatively the best possible.

The right number of children is the number that will best favor the personal development of all members of the family, at the same time taking account of the wider interests of society. Regulation of births will thus be necessary, generally speaking, but should always be inspired by a generous spirit of self-giving love in accordance with the purpose of marital fruitfulness.

If marriage is divorced from its purpose that, of course, transcends physical fruitfulness but includes it within the bounds of what is physically possible and morally responsible, its nature will also be misunderstood, and the result will be group selfishness hostile to life.

Conclusion

For all the reasons discussed, the Church teaches that marriage is intrinsically indissoluble, that is, that married people, whether Christian or not, can never abandon their own marriage and then lawfully contract a new one. The Church, however, has the right and authority to decide that an apparent marriage was fundamentally flawed from the beginning and was thus not a valid marriage, thereby annulling it. The Courts have the same authority from the State. In this case, partners would be free to enter into another marriage after sufficient maturity is attained and flaws removed.

Common life can be given up, furthermore, for grave and just reasons (separation from bed and board) so as to avoid a greater evil -- that is, if continuing to live together as befits the nature and purpose of marriage as such would, in the actual circumstances, be contrary to the dignity of either party or the good of the family or both. Such would be the case of serious abuse of a spouse or children that would endanger their health or life. But, because marriage is a total dedication that does not involve, but excludes, self-destruction, the right of the innocent party to a separation is limited by the duties of love. There must be grounds for separation so serious that it is too much to expect a person to continue common life, and the interests of the children must be safeguarded so far as possible.

--Waldemar Molinski, edited by Patrick J. Hession

PARENTS ARE CALLED TO WITNESS TO THEIR FAITH AND HOPE

Both Esther and Paul testify that the family is called to work for the handing on of the faith.

Esther admits: "Ever since I was born, I have heard, in the tribe of my family, that you, O Lord, took Israel out of all the nations" (14:5).

Paul follows the tradition of his Jewish ancestors by worshiping God with a pure conscience. He praises the sincere faith of Timothy and speaks to him about "a faith that lived first in your grandmother Lois and your mother Eunice, and now, I am sure, lives in you" (2 Timothy 1:15).

In these biblical testimonies, the family includes not only parents and children but also grandparents and ancestors. The family, thus, appears to us as a community of generations and the guarantee of a patrimony of traditions.

None of us gave ourselves life or single handedly learned how to live. All of us received from others both life itself and its basic truths, and we have been called to attain perfection in relationship and loving communion with others.

The family, founded on indissoluble marriage between a man and a woman, is the expression of this relational, filial, and communal aspect of life. It is the setting where men and women are enabled to be born with dignity and to grow and develop in an integral manner.

Once children are born, through their relationship with their parents, they begin to share in a family tradition with even older roots. Together with the gift of life, they receive a whole patrimony of experience. Parents have the right and the inalienable duty to transmit this heritage to their children: to help them find their own identity, to initiate them to the life of society, to foster the responsible exercise of their moral freedom and their ability to love on the basis of their having been loved and, above all, to enable them to encounter God.

Children experience human growth and maturity to the extent that they trustingly accept this heritage and training that they gradually make their own. They are, thus. enabled to make a personal synthesis between what has been passed on and what is new, a synthesis that every individual and generation is called to make.

At the origin of every man and woman, and, thus, in all human fatherhood and motherhood, we find God the Creator. For this reason, married couples must accept the child born to them not simply as theirs alone but also as a child of God, loved for his or her own sake and called to be a son or daughter of God. What is more: each generation, all parenthood, and every family has its origin in God, who is Father, Son, and Holy Spirit.

Esther's father had passed on to her, along with the memory of her forebears and her people, the memory of a God who is the origin of all and to whom all are called to answer. It is the memory of God the Father, who chose a people for himself and who acts in history for our salvation. The memory of this Father sheds light on our deepest human identity: where we come from, who we are, and how great is our dignity.

Certainly, we come from our parents and are their children, but we also come from God, who has created us in his image and called us to be his children. Consequently, at the origin of every human being. there is not something haphazard or chance but a loving plan of God. This was revealed to us by Jesus Christ, the true Son of God and a perfect man. He knew whence he came and whence all of us have come: from the love of his Father and our Father.

Faith, then, is not merely a cultural heritage but the constant working of the grace of God who calls and our human freedom, which can respond or not to his call. Even if no one can answer for another person, Christian parents are still called to give a credible witness of their Christian faith and hope. They need to ensure that God's call and the good news of Christ will reach their children with the utmost clarity and authenticity.

As the years pass, this gift of God that the parents have helped set before the eyes of the little ones will also need to be cultivated with wisdom and gentleness in order to instill in them a capacity for discernment. Thus, with the constant witness of the their parents' conjugal love, permeated with a living faith and with the loving accompaniment of the Christian community, children will be helped better to appropriate the gift of their faith, to discover the deepest meaning of their own lives, and to respond with joy and gratitude.

The Christian family passes on the faith when parents teach their children to pray and when they pray with them, when they lead them to the sacraments and gradually introduce them to the life of the Church; when all join in reading the Bible, letting the light of faith shine on their family life and praising God as our Father.

In contemporary culture, we often see an excessive exaltation of the freedom of the individual as an autonomous subject, as if we were self-created and self-sufficient, apart from our relationship with others and our responsibilities in their regard.

Attempts are being made to organize the life of society on the basis of subjective and ephemeral desires alone, with no reference to objective, prior truths such as the dignity of each human being and his or her inalienable rights and duties, which every social group is called to serve.

The Church does not cease to remind us that true human freedom derives from our having been created in God's image and likeness. Christian education is, consequently, an education in freedom and for freedom.

"We do not do good as slaves, who are not free to act otherwise, but we do it because we are personally responsible for the world; because we love truth and goodness, because we love God himself, and, therefore, his creatures as well. This is the true freedom to which the Holy Spirit wants to lead us (*Homily for the Vigil of Pentecost*, June 9, 2006).

Jesus Christ is the perfect human being, an example of filial freedom, who teaches us to share with others his own love: "As the Father has loved me, so I have loved you; abide in my love" (John 15:9).

And so, the Second Vatican Council teaches that "Christian married couples and parents, following their own way, should support one another in grace all through life with faithful love and should train their children, lovingly received from God, in Christian doctrine and evangelical virtues. In this way, they present to all an example of unfailing and generous love, they build up the brotherhood of charity, and they stand as witnesses and co-operators of the fruitfulness of

Mother Church, as a sign of and a share in that love with which Christ loved his Bride and gave himself for her" (*Lumen Gentium* 41).

The joyful love with which our parents welcomed us and accompanied our first steps in this world is like a sacramental sign and prolongation of the benevolent love of God from which we have come. The experience of being welcomed and loved by God and by our parents is always the firm foundation for authentic human growth and authentic development, helping us to mature on the way towards truth and love and to move beyond ourselves, in order to enter into communion with others and with God.

To help us advance along the path of human maturity, the Church teaches us to respect and foster the marvelous reality of the indissoluble marriage between man and woman, which is also the origin of the family. To recognize and assist this institution is one of the greatest services that can be rendered nowadays to the common good and to the authentic development of individuals and societies as well as the best means of ensuring the dignity, equality, and true freedom of the human person.

This being the case, I want to stress the importance and the positive role that the Church's various family associations are playing in support of marriage and the family. Consequently, "I wish to call on all Christians to collaborate cordially and courageously with all people of good will who are serving the family in accordance with their responsibility" (*Familiaris Consortio* 86) so that, by joining forces in a legitimate plurality of initiatives, they will contribute to the promotion of the authentic good of the family in contemporary society.

Let us return for a moment to the Book of Esther. The Church at prayer has seen in this humble queen, interceding with all her heart for her suffering people, a prefigurement of Mary, whom her Son has given to us all as our Mother; a prefigurement of the Mother who protects by her love God's family on its earthly pilgrimage. Mary is the image and model of all mothers, of their great mission to be guardians of life, of their mission to be teachers of the art of living and of the art of loving.

The Christian family -- father, mother and children -- is called, then, to do all these things not as a task imposed from without but rather as a gift of the sacramental grace of marriage poured out upon the spouses. If they remain open to the Spirit and implore his help, he will not fail to bestow on them the love of God the Father made manifest and incarnate in Christ.

The presence of the Spirit will help spouses not to lose sight of the source and criterion of their love and self-giving and to cooperate with him to make it visible and incarnate in every aspect of their lives.

The Spirit will also awaken in them a yearning for the definitive encounter with Christ in the house of his Father and our Father. This is the message of hope that I wish to share with all the families of the world. Amen.

--Pope Benedict XVI

CHILDREN HAVE THE RIGHT TO A HOME LIKE THAT OF NAZARETH

Human beings were created in the image and likeness of God for love, and complete human fulfillment only comes about when we make a sincere gift of ourselves to others.

The family is the privileged setting where every person learns to give and receive love. That is why the Church constantly wishes to demonstrate her pastoral concern for this reality, so basic for the human person.

"God, who is love and who created man and woman for love, has called them to love. By creating man and woman, he called them to an intimate communion of life and love in marriage. 'So they are no longer two but one flesh' (Matthew 19:6, *Catechism of the Catholic Church, Compendium* 337).

This is the truth that the Church tirelessly proclaims to the world. My beloved predecessor Pope St. John Paul II said that people have been made "in the image and likeness of God not only by being human but also by the communion of the persons that man and woman have formed since the beginning. They become the image of God not so much in their aloneness as in their communion" (*Catechesis*, 14 November 1979).

The family is an intermediate institution between individuals and society, and nothing can completely take its place. The family is itself based primarily on a deep interpersonal relationship between husband and wife, sustained by affection and mutual understanding. To enable this, it receives abundant help from God in the sacrament of Matrimony, which brings with it a true vocation to holiness.

Would that our children might experience more the harmony and affection between their parents rather than disagreements and discord since the love between father and mother is a source of great security for children and teaches them the beauty of a faithful and lasting love.

The family is a necessary good for peoples, an indispensable foundation for society, and a great and lifelong treasure for couples. It is a unique good for children, who are meant to be the fruit of the love, of the total and generous self-giving of their parents. To proclaim the whole truth about the family, based on marriage as a domestic Church and a sanctuary of life, is a great responsibility incumbent upon all.

Father and mother have said a complete "yes" in the sight of God, which constitutes the basis of the sacrament that joins them together. Likewise, for the inner relationship of the family to be complete, they also need to say a "yes" of acceptance to the children, whom they have given birth to or adopted and each of which has his or her own personality and character.

In this way, children will grow up in a climate of acceptance and love and, upon reaching sufficient maturity, will then want to say "yes" in turn to those who gave them life.

The challenges of present-day society, marked by the centrifugal forces generated especially in urban settings, make it necessary to ensure that families do not feel alone. A small family can encounter difficult obstacles when it is isolated from relatives and friends.

The ecclesial community, therefore, has the responsibility of offering support, encouragement, and spiritual nourishment that can strengthen the cohesiveness of the family, especially in times of trial or difficulty. Here, faith communities have an important role to play, as do the various ecclesial associations, called to cooperate as networks of support and a helping hand for the growth of families in faith.

Christ has shown us what is always the supreme source of our life and, thus, of the lives of families: "This is my commandment, that you love one another as I have loved you. No one had greater love than this, to lay down one's life for one's friends" (John 15:12-13).

The love of God himself has been poured out upon us in Baptism. Consequently, families are called to experience this same kind of love because the Lord makes it possible for us, through our human love, to be sensitive, loving, and merciful like Christ.

Together with passing on the faith and the love of God, one of the greatest responsibilities of families is that of training free and responsible persons. For this reason, the parents need gradually to give their children greater freedom while remaining for some time the guardians of that freedom.

If children see that their parents and, more generally, all the adults around them live life with joy and enthusiasm, despite all difficulties, they will themselves develop that profound "joy of life" that can help them to overcome wisely the inevitable obstacles and problems that are part of life. Furthermore, when families are not closed in on themselves, children come to learn that every person is worthy of love and that there is a basic, universal brotherhood that embraces every human being.

"As a mother who teacher her children to speak and so to understand and communicate, the Church, our Mother, teaches us the language of faith in order to introduce us to the understanding and the life of faith" (CCC 171). This is symbolically in the liturgy of Baptism: with the handing over of the lighted candle, the parents are made part of the mystery of new life as children of God given to their sons and daughters in the waters of Baptism.

To hand down the faith to children, with the help of individuals and institutions like the parish, the school, or Catholic associations, is a responsibility that parents cannot overlook, neglect, or completely delegate to others.

"The Christian family is called the domestic church because the family manifests and lives out the communal and familiar nature of the Church as the family of God. Each family member, in accord with his or her own role, exercises the baptismal priesthood and contributes towards making the family a community of grace and of prayer, a school of human and Christian virtues, and the place where the faith is first proclaimed to children" (*Catechism of the Catholic Church, Compendium*, 350).

What is more: "Parents, in virtue of their participation in the fatherhood of God, have the first responsibility for the education of their children, and they are the first heralds of the faith for them. They have the duty to love and respect their children as persons and as children of God ... in particular, they have the mission of educating their children in the Christian faith" (ibid, 460).

The language of faith is learned in homes, where this faith grows and is strengthened through prayer and Christian practice. In Deuteronomy, we have the prayer constantly repeated by the Chosen People, the "Shema Israel," which Jesus himself would have heard and recited in his home in Nazareth. He himself would refer to it during his public life, as we see in the Gospel of Mark (12:29).

This is the faith of the Church that is born of God's love, that comes through your families. To live the fullness of this faith, in all its wondrous newness, is a great gift. All the same, at those times when God's face seems to be hidden, believing can be difficult and takes great effort.

Proclaiming the Gospel of the family, reaffirming the strength and identity of the family founded upon marriage and open to the generous gift of life, where children are accompanied in their bodily and spiritual growth, is the best way to counter a widespread hedonism that reduces human relations to banality and empties them of their authentic value and beauty. To promote the values of marriage does not stand in the way of fully experiencing the happiness that man and women encounter in their mutual love.

Christian faith and ethics are not meant to stifle love but to make it healthier, stronger, and more truly free. Human love needs to be purified and to mature if it is to be fully human and the principle of a true and lasting joy (cf. *Address at Saint John Lateran*, June 5, 2006).

And so, I invite government leaders and legislators to reflect on the evident benefits that homes in peace and harmony assure to individuals and the family, the neuralgic center of society, as the Holy See has stated in the Charter of the Rights of the Family.

The purpose of laws is the integral good of persons in response to their needs and aspirations. This good is a significant help to society, of which it cannot be deprived, and, for peoples, a safeguard and a purification.

The family is also a school that enables men and women to grow to the full measure of their humanity. The experience of being loved by their parents helps children to become aware of their dignity as children.

Children need to be brought up in the faith, to be loved and protected. Along with their basic right to be born and to be raised in the faith, children also have the right to a home, which takes as its model the home of Nazareth, and to be shielded from all dangers and threats.

I would now like to say a word to grandparents, who are so important for every family. They can be, and so often are, the guarantors of the affection and tenderness that every human being needs to give and receive. They offer little ones the perspective of time, they are memory and richness of families. In no way should they ever be excluded from the family circle. They are a treasure which the younger generation should not be denied, especially when they bear witness to their faith at the approach of death.

O God, who in the Holy Family left us a perfect model of family life lived in faith and obedience to your will, help us to be examples of faith and love for your commandments. Help us in our mission of transmitting the faith that we received from our parents. Open the hearts of our children so that the seed of faith, which they received in Baptism, will grow in them. Strengthen the faith of our young people, that they may grow in knowledge of Jesus. Increase love and faithfulness in all marriages, especially those going through times of suffering or difficulty. United to Joseph and Mary, we ask this through Jesus Christ your Son, our Lord. Amen.

--Pope Benedict XVI

THE FAMILY AND THE GOOD NEWS (Luke 2:6-14)

The Church as Mother gives birth to, educates, and builds up the Christian family. By proclaiming the Word of God, the Church reveals to the Christian family its true identity, what it is and should be according to the Lord's plan; by celebrating the sacraments, the Church enriches and strengthens the Christian family with the grace of Christ; by the continuous proclamation of love, the Church encourages and guides the Christian family to the service of love so that it may imitate and relive the same self-giving and sacrificial love that the Lord Jesus Christ has for the entire race.

In turn, the Christian family is grafted into the mystery of the Church to such a degree as to become a sharer, in its own way, in the saving mission proper to the Church. The Christian family welcomes and announces the Word of God; it thus becomes more and more each day a believing and evangelizing community.

Christian spouses and parents are required to offer the obedience of faith (cf. Romans 16:26). They are called upon to welcome the word of the Lord that reveals to them the marvelous news, the Good News of their conjugal and family life sanctified and made a source of sanctity by Christ himself. Only in faith can they discover and admire with joyful gratitude the dignity to which God has deigned to raise marriage and the family, making them a sign and meeting place of the loving covenant between Jesus Christ and his bride, the Church.

The very preparation for Christian marriage is itself a journey of faith. It is a special opportunity for the engaged couple to rediscover and deepen the faith received in Baptism and nourished by their Christian upbringing. In this way, they come to recognize and freely accept their vocation to follow Christ and to serve the kingdom of God in the married state.

The celebration of the sacrament of marriage is the basic moment of the faith of the couple. This sacrament, in essence, is the proclamation in the Church of the Good News concerning married love. It is the Word of God that "reveals" and "fulfills" the wise and loving plan of God for the married couple, giving them a mysterious and real share in the very love with which God himself loves humanity. The sacramental celebration of marriage is a proclamation of the Word of God that is made within and with the Church as a community of believers. This also requires that it be prolonged in the life of the married couple and of the family. God, who called the couple to marriage, continues to call them in marriage. In and through the events, problems, difficulties, and circumstances of everyday life, God comes to them, revealing and presenting the concrete demands of their sharing in the love of Christ for his Church in the particular family, social, and ecclesial situation in which they find themselves.

To the extent in which the Christian family accepts the Gospel and matures in faith, it becomes an evangelizing community. The family, like the Church, ought to be a place where the Gospel is transmitted and from which the Gospel radiates. In a family that is conscious of this mission, all the members evangelize and are evangelized. The parents not only communicate the Gospel to their children, but from their children they can themselves receive the same Gospel as deeply lived by them. And, such a family becomes the evangelizer of many other families and of the neighborhood of which it forms a part.

One cannot fail to stress the evangelizing action of the family in the evangelizing apostolate of the laity. In fact, the future of evangelization depends in great part on the Church of the home. This apostolic mission of the family is rooted in baptism and receives from the grace of the sacrament of marriage new strength to transmit the faith, to sanctify and transform our present society according to God's plan. The future of humanity lies in the hands of the families that are strong enough to provide coming generations with reasons for living.

CHRISTIAN FAMILY: WITNESS TO THE PASCAL COVENANT (Ephesians 5:25-33)

Particularly today, the Christian family has a special vocation to witness to the paschal covenant of Christ by constantly radiating the joy of love and the certainty of the hope for which it must give an account: the Christian family loudly proclaims both the present virtues of the kingdom of God and the hope of a blessed life to come.

The Church professes that marriage, as the sacrament of the covenant between husband and wife, is a "great mystery" because it expresses the spousal love of Christ for his Church. St. Paul writes, "Husbands, love your wives as Christ lived the Church and gave himself up for her that he might sanctify her, having cleansed her by the washing of water with the word" (Ephesians 5:25-26). The apostle is speaking here about Baptism, which he discusses at length in the Letter to the Romans, where he presents it as a sharing in the death of Christ leading to a sharing in his life (cf. Romans 6:3-4). In this sacrament, the believer is born as a new man, for Baptism has the power to communicate new life, the very life of God. The mystery of the God-man is in some way recapitulated in the event of Baptism. As St. Irenaeus would later say, along with many other Fathers of the Church of both East and West, "Christ Jesus, our Lord, the Son of God, became the son of man so that man could become a son of God" (Cf. *Adversus haereses*, III, 10, 2; PG 7, 873).

There is unquestionably a new presentation of the eternal truth about marriage and the family in the light of the New Covenant. Christ has revealed this truth in the Gospel by his presence at Cana in Galilee, by the sacrifice of the Cross, and by the sacraments of his Church. Husbands and wives, thus, discover in Christ the point of reference for their spousal love. In speaking of Christ as the Bridegroom of the Church, St. Paul uses the analogy of spousal love, referring back to the Book of Genesis, "A man leaves his father and his mother and cleaves to his wife, and they become one flesh" (Genesis 2:24). This is the "great mystery" of that eternal love already present in creation, revealed in Christ, and entrusted to the Church. "This mystery is a profound one," the apostle repeats, "and I am saying that it refers to Christ and the Church" (Ephesians 5:32).

The Church cannot, therefore, be understood as the mystical Body of Christ, as the sign of man's covenant with God in Christ, or as the universal sacrament of salvation unless we keep in mind the "great mystery" involved in the creation of man as male and female and the vocation of both to conjugal love, to fatherhood and to motherhood. The "great mystery," which is the Church and humanity in Christ, does not exist apart from the "great mystery" expressed in the "one flesh" (cf. Genesis 2:24; Ephesians 5:31 &32), that is, in the reality of marriage and the family.

The family itself is the great mystery of God. As the "domestic church," it is the bride of Christ. The universal Church, and every particular Church in her, is most immediately revealed as the Bride of Christ in the "domestic church" and in its experience of love: conjugal love, paternal and maternal love, fraternal love, the love of a community of persons and of generations. Could we even imagine human love without the Bridegroom and the love with which he first loved to the end? Only if husbands and wives share in that love and in that "great mystery" can they love "to the end." Unless they share in it, they do not know "to the end" what love truly is and how radical are its demands.

THE FAMILY: HEART OF EVANGELIZATION

Among the fundamental tasks of the Christian family is its ecclesial task: The family is placed at the service of building up the kingdom of God in history by participating in the live and mission of the Church. The Christian family is called upon to take part actively and responsibly in the mission of the Church in a way that is original and specific, by placing itself, in what it is and what it does, as an intimate community of life and love, at the service of the Church and of society.

Since the Christian family is a community in which the relationships are renewed by Christ through faith and the sacraments, the family's sharing in the Church's mission should follow a community pattern: The spouses together as a couple, the parents and children as a family, must live their service to the Church and to the world. They must be "of one heart and soul" (cf. Acts 4:32) in faith, through the shared apostolic zeal that animates them, and through their shared commitment to works of service to the ecclesial and civil communities.

The Christian family also builds up the kingdom of God in history through the everyday realities that concern and distinguish its state of life. It is, thus, in the love between husband and wife and among the members of the family, a love lived out in all its extraordinary richness of values and demands: totality, oneness, fidelity, and fruitfulness, that the Christian family's participation in the prophetic, priestly, and kingly mission of Jesus Christ and of his Church finds expression and realization. Therefore, love and life constitute the nucleus of the saving mission of the Christian family in the Church and for the Church.

Thus, the Christian family, which springs from marriage as a reflection of the loving covenant uniting Christ with the Church, and as a participation in that covenant will manifest to all people the Savior's living presence in the world, and the genuine nature of the Church. This the family will do by the mutual love of the spouses, by their generous fruitfulness, their solidarity and faithfulness, and by the loving way in which all the members of the family work together.

By sharing in her life and mission, the family is called to carry out its task of education in the Church. She wishes to carry out her educational mission above all through families who are made capable of undertaking this task by the sacrament of matrimony, through the "grace of state" which follows from it and the specific "charism" proper to the entire family community.

Certainly one area in which the family has an irreplaceable role is that of religious education, which enables the family to grow as a "domestic church." Religious education and the catechesis of children make the family a true subject of evangelization and the apostolate within the Church. We are speaking or a right intrinsically linked to the principle of religious liberty. Families, and more specifically parents, are free to choose for their children a particular kind of religious and moral education consonant with their own convictions. Even when they entrust these responsibilities to ecclesiastical institutions or to schools administered by religious personnel, their educational presence ought to continue to be constant and active.

THE CHRISTIAN FAMILY: THE DOMESTIC CHURCH

Christ chose to be born and to grow up in the bosom of the holy family of Joseph and Mary. The Church is nothing other than "the family of God." From the beginning, the core of the Church was often constituted by those who had become believers "together with all [their] household" (cf. Acts 18:8). When they were converted, they desired that their whole household should also be saved (cf. Acts 16:31 and 11:14). These families who became believers were islands of Christian life in an unbelieving world.

In our own time, in a world often alien and even hostile to faith, believing families are of primary importance as centers of living, radiant faith. It is in the bosom of the family that parents are by word and example the first heralds of the faith with regard to their children. They should encourage them in the vocation that is proper to each child, fostering with special care any religious vocation.

It is here that the father of the family, the mother, children, and all members of the family exercise the priesthood of the baptized in a privileged way by the reception of the sacraments, prayer and thanksgiving, the witness of a holy life, and self-denial and active charity. Thus, the home is the first school of Christian life and a school for human enrichment. Here, one learns endurance and the joy of work, fraternal love, generous, even repeated, forgiveness, and, above all, divine worship in prayer and the offering of one's life.

The absolute need for family catechesis emerges with particular force in certain situations that the Church unfortunately experiences in some places. In places where anti-religious legislation endeavors even to prevent education in the faith, and in places where widespread unbelief or invasive secularism makes real religious growth practically impossible, "the Church of the home" remains the one place where children and young people can receive an authentic catechesis.

The family is the domestic church that is also called to be a luminous sign of the presence of Christ and of his love for those who are "far away," for families who do not yet believe, and for those Christian families who no longer live in accordance with the faith that they once received.

The Christian family is called to enlighten by its example and its witness those who seek the truth.

Just like Aquila and Priscilla (cf. Acts 18; Romans 16:3 & 4) at the dawn of Christianity, today the Church shows forth her perennial newness and fruitfulness by the presence of Christian couples and families who dedicate at least a part of their lives to working in missionary territories, proclaiming the Gospel and doing service to their fellowmen in the love of Jesus Christ.

Many single people remain without a human family often due to conditions of poverty. Some live their situation in the spirit of the Beatitudes, serving God and neighbor in exemplary fashion. The doors of homes, the "domestic churches," and of the great family, which is the Church must be open to all of them. No one is without a family in this world: the Church is a home and family for everyone, especially those who "labor and are heavy laden" (Matthew 11:28).

THE HOLINESS OF THE FAMILY AT THE SERVICE OF THE GOSPEL (Mark 16:14-18)

By means of the sacrament of marriage, in which it is rooted and from which it draws its nourishment, the family is continuously vivified by the Lord Jesus and called and engaged by him in a dialogue with God through the sacraments, through the offering of one's life, and through prayer.

The sacrament of marriage is the specific source and original means of sanctification for Christian married couples and families. It takes up again and makes specific the sanctifying grace of Baptism. By virtue of the mystery of the death and Resurrection of Christ, of which the spouses are made part in a new way by marriage, conjugal love is purified and made holy: This love the Lord has judged worthy of special gifts, healing, perfecting, and exalting gifts of grace and of charity.

The gift of Jesus Christ is not exhausted in the actual celebration of the sacrament of marriage but rather accompanies the married couple throughout their lives. Jesus Christ abides with them so that, just as he loved the Church and handed himself over on her behalf, the spouses may love each other with perpetual fidelity through mutual self-dedication. For this reason, Christian spouses have a special sacrament by which they are fortified and receive a kind of consecration in the duties and dignity of their state. By virtue of this sacrament, as spouses fulfill their conjugal and family obligations, they are penetrated with the spirit of Christ, who fills their whole lives with faith, hope, and charity. Thus, they increasingly advance toward their own perfection, as well as toward their mutual sanctification, and hence contribute jointly to the glory of God.

Christian spouses and parents are included in the universal call to sanctity. For them, this call is specified by the sacrament they have celebrated and is carried out concretely in the realities proper to their conjugal and family life. This gives rise to the grace and requirement of an authentic and profound conjugal and family spirituality that draws its inspiration from the themes of creation, covenant, cross, resurrection, and sign.

Just as husbands and wives receive from the sacrament the gift and responsibility of translating into daily living the sanctification bestowed on them, so the same sacrament confers on them the grace and moral obligation of transforming their whole lives into a "spiritual sacrifice."

In our age, as in the past, there is no lack of witness to the "gospel of the family," even if they are not well known or have not been proclaimed saints by the Church. In the Church, the treasure of the family has been entrusted first and foremost to witnesses: to those fathers and mothers, sons and daughters who, through the family, have discovered the path of their human and Christian vocation, the dimension of the "inner man" (Ephesians 3:16) of which the apostle Paul speaks, and, thus, have attained holiness. The Holy Family is the beginning of countless other holy families. And, holiness is the vocation of all the baptized.

THE EUCHARIST: SIGN AND NOURISHMENT FOR UNCONDITIONAL CONJUGAL LOVE (John 6:53-58)

The sacraments of Christian initiation - Baptism, Confirmation, and the Eucharist - lay the foundations of every Christian life. The sharing in the divine nature, given to people through the grace of Christ, bears a certain likeness to the origin, development, and nourishing of natural life. The faithful are born anew by Baptism, strengthened by the sacrament of Confirmation, and receive in the Eucharist the food of eternal life. By means of these sacraments of Christian initiation, they, thus, receive in increasing measure the treasures of the divine life and advance toward the perfection of charity.

The Sunday Eucharist, which every week gathers Christians together as God's family round the table of the Word and the Bread of Life, is also the most natural antidote to dispersion. It is the privileged place where communion is ceaselessly proclaimed and nurtured. Precisely through sharing in the Eucharist, the Lord's Day also becomes the Day of the Church.

The Christian family's sanctifying role is grounded in Baptism and has its highest expression in the Eucharist, to which Christian marriage is intimately connected. The Eucharist is the very source of Christian marriage. The Eucharistic sacrifice, in fact, represents Christ's covenant of love with the Church, sealed with his Blood on the Cross (cf. John 19:34). In this sacrifice of the new and eternal covenant, Christian spouses encounter the source from which their own marriage covenant flows, is interiorly structured and continuously renewed. As a representation of Christ's sacrifice of love for the Church, the Eucharist is a fountain of charity. In the Eucharistic gift of charity, the Christian family finds the foundation and soul of its "communion" and its "mission": by partaking in the Eucharistic bread, the different members of the Christian family become one body, which reveals and shares in the wider unity of the Church. Their sharing in the Body of Christ that is "given up" and in his Blood that is "shed" becomes a never-ending source of missionary and apostolic dynamism for the Christian family.

The Eucharist is truly a wondrous sacrament. In it, Christ has given us himself as food and drink, as a source of saving power. He has left himself to us that we might have life and have it in abundance (cf. John 10:10): the life which is in him and which he has shared with us by the gift of the Spirit in rising from the dead on the third day. The life that comes from Christ is a life for us. Christ is close to you. He is Emmanuel, God with us, in an even greater way whenever you approach the table of the Eucharist. It can happen, as it did at Emmaus, that he is recognized only in "the breaking of the bread" (cf. Luke 24:35). It may well be that he has been knocking at the door for a long time, waiting for it to be opened so that he can enter and eat with us (cf. Revelation 3:20).

The Last Supper and the words he spoke there contain all the power and wisdom of the sacrifice of the Cross. No other power and wisdom exist by which we can be saved and through which we can help to save others. There is no other power and no other wisdom by which you, parents, can educate both your children and yourselves. The educational power of the Eucharist has been proved down the generations and centuries.

RECONCILIATION AND FORGIVENESS IN THE FAMILY (Ephesians 2:13-18)

An essential and permanent part of the Christian family's sanctifying role consists in accepting the call to conversion that the Gospel addresses to all Christians, who do not always remain faithful to the "newness" of Baptism that makes them "saints."

Often refusing to acknowledge God as their beginning, people have disrupted also their proper relationship to their own ultimate goal as wall as their whole relationship toward themselves, others, and all created things. The Christian family, too, is sometimes unfaithful to the law of Baptismal grace and holiness proclaimed anew in the sacrament of Marriage.

Family communion can only be preserved and perfected through a great spirit of sacrifice. It requires, in fact, a ready and generous openness of each and all to understanding, to forbearance, to pardon, to reconciliation. There is no family that does not know how selfishness, discord, tension, and conflict violently attack and at times mortally wound its own communion. Hence, there arise the many and varied forms of division in family life. At the same time, every family is called by the God of peace to have the joyous and renewing experience of "reconciliation," that is, communion re-established, unity restored. In particular, participation in the sacrament of Reconciliation and in the banquet of the one Body of Christ offers to the Christian family the grace and the responsibility of overcoming every division and of moving toward the fullness of communion willed by God, responding in this way to the ardent desire of the Lord: "that they may be one." (John 17:21)

This capacity depends on the divine grace of forgiveness and reconciliation, which always ensures the spiritual energy to begin anew. For this very reason, family members need to encounter Christ in the Church through the wonderful sacrament of Penance and Reconciliation.

Repentance and mutual pardon within the bosom of the Christian family, so much a part of daily life, receive their specific sacramental expression in Christian penance. Pope Pius VI wrote of married couples: "If sin should still keep its hold over them, let them not be discouraged but, rather, have recourse with humble perseverance to the mercy of God, which is abundantly poured forth in the sacrament of Penance."

It is necessary to rediscover Christ as the "mystery of piety," the one in whom God shows us his compassionate heart and reconciles us fully with himself. It is this face of Christ that must be rediscovered through the sacrament of Penance, which, for the faithful, is the ordinary way of obtaining forgiveness and the remission of serious sins committed after Baptism. The celebration of this sacrament acquires special significance for family life. While they discover in faith that sin contradicts not only the covenant with God but also the covenant between husband and wife and the communion of the family, the married couple and the other members of the family are led to an encounter with God, who is "rich in mercy" (Ephesians 2:4) and who bestows on them his love that is more powerful than sin and who reconstructs and brings to perfection the marriage covenant and the family communion.

THE FAMILY: A COMMUNITY OF PRAYER (Matthew 7:7-11)

Prayer makes the Son of God present among us. The words with which the Lord Jesus promises his presence can be applied to the members of the Christian family in a special way: "Again I say to you, if two of you agree on earth about anything they ask, it will be done for them by my Father in Heaven. Where two or three are gathered in my Name, there am I in the midst of them" (Matthew 18:19-20)

In effect, the Baptismal priesthood of the faithful, exercised in the sacrament of Marriage, constitutes the basis of a mission for the spouses and the family by which their daily lives are transformed into "spiritual sacrifices acceptable to God through Jesus Christ" (1 Peter 2:5). The Christian communities must become genuine "schools of prayer," where the meeting with Christ is expressed not just in imploring help but also in thanksgiving, praise, adoration, contemplation, listening, and ardent devotion until the heart truly "falls in love." Intense prayer, yes, but it does not distract us from our commitment to history. By opening our heart to the love of God, it also opens it to the love of our brothers and sisters and makes us capable of shaping history according to God's plan.

Christian parents have the specific responsibility of educating their children in prayer, introducing them to a gradual discovery of the mystery of God and to personal dialogue with him. It is particularly in the Christian family, enriched by the grace and the office of the sacrament of matrimony, that children should be taught from the earliest years, according to the faith received in Baptism, to know God, to worship him, and to love their neighbor.

Family prayer has its own characteristic qualities. It is prayer offered in common, husband and wife together, parents and children together. Communion in prayer is both a consequence of and a requirement for the communion bestowed by the sacraments of Baptism and Matrimony. The concrete example and living witness of parents is fundamental and irreplaceable in educating their children to pray. Only by praying together with their children can a father and mother, exercising their royal priesthood, penetrate the innermost depths of their children's hearts and leave an impression that the future events in their lives will not be able to destroy.

It is significant that precisely in and through prayer people come to discover in a very simple and yet profound way their own unique subjectivity. In prayer, the human "I" more easily perceives the depth of what it means to be a person. This is also true of the family, which is not only the basic "cell" of society but also possesses a particular subjectivity of its own. This subjectivity finds its first and fundamental confirmation, and is strengthened, precisely when the members of the family meet in the common invocation, "Our Father." Prayer increases the strength and spiritual unity of the family, helping it to partake of God's own "strength."

An important purpose of the prayer of the domestic Church is to serve as the natural introduction for the children to the liturgical prayer of the whole Church. Hence, there is the need for gradual participation by all the members of the Christian family in the celebration of the Eucharist and of the other sacraments, particularly the sacraments of Christian initiation of the children. The liturgy is the summit toward which the activity of the Church is directed. It is also the source from which all her power flows. It is, therefore, the privileged place for catechizing the people of God. Catechesis is intrinsically linked with the whole of liturgical and sacramental activity because it is in the sacraments, especially in the Eucharist, that Christ Jesus works in fullness for the transformation of people.

THE FAMILY: NUCLEUS AND SOURCE OF SOCIAL GOOD - (Acts 2:42-47)

The family has vital and organic links with society since it is its foundation and nourishes it continually through its role of service to life. It is from the family that citizens come to birth. It is also within the family that they find the first school of the social virtues that are the animating principle of the existence and development of society itself. Thus, far from being closed in on itself, the family is, by nature and vocation, open to other families and to society, and undertakes its social role.

The family is, in fact, a community of persons whose proper way of existing and living together is communion, communion of persons. Therefore, the family is the first and fundamental school of social living. As a community of love, it finds its self-giving the law that guides it and makes it grow. The self-giving that inspires the love of husband and wife for each other is the model and norm for the self-giving that must be practiced in the relationships between brothers and sisters and the different generations living together in the family. And, the communion and sharing that are part of everyday life in the home at times of joy and at times of difficulty are the most concrete and effective instruction for the active, responsible, and fruitful inclusion of the children in the wider horizon of society.

Every child is a gift to his or her brothers, sisters, parents, and entire family. The child's life becomes a gift for the very people who were givers of this life and who cannot help but feel its presence, its sharing in their life, and its contribution to their common good and to the good of the community of the family. This truth is obvious in its simplicity and profundity, whatever the complexity and even the possible pathology of the psychological makeup of certain persons. The common good of the whole of society dwells in man; he is "the way of the Church."

The very existence of communion and sharing that should characterize the family's daily life represents its first and fundamental contribution to society. The relationships between the members of the family community are inspired and guided by the law of "free giving." By respecting and fostering personal dignity in each and every one as the only basis for value, this free giving takes the form of heartfelt acceptance, encounter and dialogue, disinterested availability, generous service, and deep solidarity.

Thus, the fostering of authentic and mature communion between persons within the family is the first and irreplaceable school of social life, an example and stimulus for the broader community relationships marked by respect, justice, dialogue, and love. The family is, thus, the place of origin and the most effective means for humanizing and personalizing society. It makes an original contribution in depth to building up the world by making possible a life that is properly speaking "human," in particular by guarding and transmitting virtues and values.

Consequently, faced with a society that is running the risk of becoming more and more depersonalized and standardized and, therefore, inhuman and dehumanizing, with the negative results of many forms of escapism, such as alcoholism, drugs, and even terrorism, the family possesses and continues still to release formidable energies. These energies are capable of taking people out of their anonymity, keeping them conscious of their personal dignity, enriching them with deep humanity, and placing them, in their uniqueness and un-repeatability, within the fabric of society.

Solidarity also needs to be practiced through participation in social and political life. Serving the Gospel of Life, thus, means that the family, particularly through its membership in family associations, works to ensure that the laws and institutions of the state in no way violate the right to life, from conception to natural death, but rather protect and promote it.

The Charter of the Rights of the Family presented to the United Nations by the Holy See in 1983 is also directed to the families themselves. It aims at reinforcing among families an awareness of the irreplaceable role and position of the family. It wishes to inspire families to unite in the defense and promotion of their rights. It encourages families to fulfill their duties in such a way that the role of the family will become more clearly appreciated and recognized in today's world.

THE FAMILY AND LOVE FOR THE WEAKEST - Matthew 15:29-39

The social role of the family certainly cannot stop short at procreation and education, even if this constitutes its primary and irreplaceable form of expression. Families, therefore, either singly or in association, can and should devote themselves to manifold social service activities, especially in favor of the poor or, at any rate, for the benefit of all people and situations that cannot be reached by the public authorities' welfare organization. The social contribution of the family has an original character, one that should be given greater recognition and more decisive encouragement, especially as the children grow up, and actually involving all its members as much as possible.

Inspired and sustained by the new commandment of love, the Christian family welcomes, respects, and serves every human being, considering each one in his or her dignity as a person and as a child of God. Love too goes beyond our brothers and sisters of the same faith since "everybody is my brother or sister." In each individual, especially in the poor, the weak, and those who suffer or are unjustly treated, love knows how to discover the face of Christ, and discover a fellow human being to be loved and served.

The Christian family places itself at the service of the human person and the world, really bringing about "human advancement." Another task for the family is to form persons in love and also to practice love in all its relationships so that it does not live closed in on itself but remains open to the community, moved by a sense of justice and concern for others, as well as by a consciousness of its responsibility toward the whole of society.

In particular, note must be taken of the ever greater importance in our society of hospitality in all its forms, from opening the door of one's home and still more of one's heart to the pleas of one's brothers and sisters, to concrete efforts to ensure that every family has its own home, as the natural environment that preserves it and makes it grow. In a special way, the Christian family is called upon to listen to St. Paul's recommendation: "Practice hospitality" (Romans 12:13). Imitating Christ's example and sharing in his love, the family must welcome the brother or sister in need: "Whoever gives to one of these little ones even a cup of cold water because he is a disciple, truly, I say to you, he shall not lose his reward" (Matthew 10:42).

The unjust distribution of wealth between the developed and developing world and between rich and poor in the same country, the misuse of natural resources consumed by the few, mass illiteracy, the continuance and re-emergence of conflict, and armed conflicts generally are also having a devastating effect on the family.

The service to the Gospel of Life is expressed in solidarity. A particularly significant expression is a willingness to adopt or take in children abandoned by their parents or in situations of serious hardship. True parental love is ready to go beyond the bonds of flesh and blood to accept children from other families, offering them whatever is necessary for their well-being and full development.

The Fathers of the Church have spoken of the family as a "domestic church," a "little church." It is called "to be together" as a family, to be for one another, to make room in a community for affirming each person as such, for affirming "this" individual person. At times, it is a matter of people with physical or psychological handicaps, of whom the so-called "progressive" society would prefer to be free. Even the family can end up like this kind of society. It does so when it hastily rids itself of people who are aged, disabled, or sick. This happens when there is a loss of faith in that God for whom "all live" (cf. Luke 20:38) and are called to the fullness of life.

THE FAMILY: SANCTUARY OF LIFE (John 10:10-15)

The fundamental task of the family is to serve life, to actualize in history the original blessing of the Creator -- that of transmitting by procreation the divine image from person to person (cf. Genesis 5:1-3).

The family has a decisive responsibility that flows from its very nature as a community of life and love, founded upon marriage, and from its mission to guard, reveal, and communicate love. Here, it is a matter of God's own love, of which parents are co-workers and, as it were, interpreters when they transmit life and raise it according to his fatherly plan. This is the love that becomes selflessness, receptiveness, and gift. Within the family, each member is accepted, respected, and honored precisely because he or she is a person; and, if any family member is in greater need, the care which he or she receives is all the more intense and attentive.

The family has a special role to play throughout the life of its members, from birth to death. It is truly the sanctuary of life: the place in which life, the gift of God, can be properly welcomed and protected against the many attacks to which it is exposed, and can develop in accordance with what constitutes authentic human growth. Consequently, the role of the family in building a culture of life is decisive and irreplaceable.

As the domestic Church, the family is summoned to proclaim, celebrate, and serve the Gospel of Life. This is a responsibility that first concerns married couples. They are called to be givers of life on the basis of an ever-greater awareness of the meaning of procreation as a unique event that clearly reveals human life as a gift received in order then to be given as a gift. In giving origin to a new life, parents recognize that the child, as the fruit of their mutual gift of love, is, in turn, a gift for both of them, a gift that flows from them.

It is above all in raising children that the family fulfills its mission to proclaim the Gospel of Life. By word and example, in the daily round of relationships and choices, and through concrete actions and signs, parents lead their children to authentic freedom, actualized in the sincere gift of self, and they cultivate in them respect for others, a sense of justice, cordial openness, dialogue, generous service, solidarity, and all the other values that help people to live life as a gift.

Even amid the difficulties of the work of education, difficulties that are often greater today, parents must trustingly and courageously train their children in the essential values of human life. Children must grow up with a correct attitude of freedom regarding material goods by adopting a simple and austere lifestyle and being fully convinced that a person is more precious for what he or she is than for what he or she has.

In raising children, Christian parents must be concerned about their children's faith and help them to fulfill the vocation that God has given them. The parents' mission as educators also includes teaching and giving their children an example of the true meaning of suffering and death. They will be able to do this if they are sensitive to all kinds of suffering around them and, even more, if they succeed in fostering attitudes of closeness, assistance, and sharing toward sick or elderly members of the family.

THE FAMILY PREPARES AND FOLLOWS YOUNG FAMILIES (John 4:43-53)

Preparing young people for marriage and family is necessary in our times. In some countries, it is still the families themselves that, according to ancient customs, ensure the passing on to young people of the values concerning married and family life. They do this through a gradual process of education or initiation. But, the changes that have taken place within almost all modern societies demand that not only the family but also the Church should be involved in the effort.

The Church has made notable efforts to promote marriage preparation, for example, by offering courses for engaged couples. All this is worthwhile and necessary. But, it must not be forgotten that preparing young people for future life as a couple is above all the task of the family. To be sure, only spiritually mature families can adequately assume that responsibility. Hence, we should point out the need for a special solidarity among families. This can be expressed in various practical ways as, for example, by associations of families for families. The institution of the family is strengthened by such expressions of solidarity, which bring together not only individuals but also communities, with a commitment to pray together and to seek together the answers to life's essential questions. Is this not an invaluable expression of the apostolate of families to one another? It is important that families attempt to build bonds of solidarity among themselves. This allows them to assist each other in the educational enterprise: parents educate other parents, and children other children. Thus, a particular tradition of education is created that draws strength from the character of the "domestic church" proper to the family.

This holds true especially for young families, which, finding themselves in a context of new values and responsibilities, are more vulnerable, especially in the first years of marriage, to possible difficulties, such as those created by adaptation to life together or by the birth of children. Young married couples should learn to accept willingly, and make good use of, the discreet, tactful, and generous help offered by other couples that already have more experience of married and family life. Thus, within the ecclesial community -- the great family made up of Christian families -- there will take place a mutual exchange of presence and help among all the families, each one putting at the service of others its own experience of life, as well as the gifts of faith and grace. Animated by a true apostolic spirit, this assistance from family to family will constitute one of the simplest, most effective, and most accessible means for transmitting from one to another those Christian values that are both the starting point and goal of all pastoral care. Thus, young families will not limit themselves merely to receiving, but in their turn, having been helped in this way, will become a source of enrichment for other longer established families through their witness of life and practical contributions.

In her pastoral care of young families, the Church must also pay special attention to helping them to live married love responsibly in relationship with its demands of communion and service to life. The Church must likewise help them to harmonize the intimacy of home life with the generous shared work of building up the Church and society.

When children are born, and the married couple becomes a family in the full and specific sense, the Church will still remain close to the parents in order that they may accept their children and love them as a gift received from the Lord of life, and joyfully accept the task of serving them in their human and Christian growth.

--Pontifical Council For The Family

CHAPTER III

THE CHRISTIAN FAMILY - LEADERSHIP OF LOVE

How To Love Your Potential Wife

In Chapter 10 of John's Gospel, Jesus says, "I am the good shepherd, and the good shepherd gives up his life for his sheep. Hired workers are not like the shepherd. They don't own the sheep, and when they see a wolf coming, they run off and leave the sheep. Then, the wolf attacks and scatters the flock. Hired workers run away because they don't care about the sheep.

"I am the good shepherd. I know my sheep, and they know me. Just as the Father knows me, I know the Father, and I give up my life for my sheep." John 10:11-15

How are you to be the shepherd of your future family that Jesus calls you to be? As always, you must look to Jesus. The secret of Jesus' success was that he only did what he saw the Father doing. In the same way, you will need to keep reminding yourself that it is Jesus who is the good shepherd. He is doing the work through his Spirit whom he has sent. Your job is to do what he is going--what you see him doing. And, what is it that the good shepherd is doing that he wants you to do? He tells you in his Word, and it starts with your potential wife and family.

You must exhibit an active commitment to and a personal relationship with your Lord and Savior, Jesus Christ. We saw this in the first session of this workbook.

You must then develop and exhibit spiritual maturity. Your teaching and leadership ability must be tested and proven in your own family that allows for growth and maturity in your future wife and children.

You must be a good father model. You should be serious, straightforward, truthful, just, holy, modest, a lover of goodness, irreproachable and blameless, of steady, even temper, a man of peace, self-controlled, gentle and not violent, not contentious or self-willed, not someone who loves money, not given to greed, hospitable, a faithful husband, a good manager of your own household, able to keep your children, if you have any, under control without sacrificing yoiur dignity, a father of children who are believers and who are not known to be wild or insubordinate, a good teacher who holds fast to authentic doctrine, well thought of by those outside the community of believers. 1 Timothy 3:2-7; Titus 1:6-9

These are the Scriptural requirements for spiritual leaders in the Church, and you should not be in a responsible position of leadership in the Church if you do not meet them or are not striving for them. These requirements should be your goals as a husband and father as you provide leadership over your family.

It is important for you to understand the fundamental Scriptural truth about your position and role in your potential family: God sets you in leadership over your wife and children, and he will hold you responsible for that leadership. You will either lead them toward God or you will lead them away from him. You will lead them in love or you will lead them in the way of your own selfishness.

Here are sixteen steps that will help you provide spiritual leadership for your future family:

1. Set an example: Practice first what you preach and expect. You can not require a behavior from your potential wife and/or children that you are not willing to require of yourself. This would be a double standard that would not honor God or them.
2. Make sound and timely decisions based upon the Scriptures and the will of God.
3. Pursue your responsibility and take responsibility for your actions. When you are wrong, ask God's forgiveness and direction. By the way, when was the last time you said you were wrong and asked for forgiveness? There is a transaction in this: when you have wronged your potential wife and/or children in word or action, tell them "I am sorry. Will you please forgive me?" They, then, need to say to you, "Yes, I forgive you." To which you reply, "Thank you." This transaction is important for all those involved in a hurt but especially in a marriage and family.
4. Commit yourself totally to your potential wife and/or children even if it means dying for them. Their security requires that they know that you will do this.
5. Gather together the children that the Lord may bring into your home and carry them in your arms, emotionally and spiritually, until they are strong enough to walk alone.
6. Pray and intercede for your potential wife and future children and stand against all the forces of Satan that would attack or infiltrate your future family. If you don't know how, find a spiritual director who can teach you.
7. Protect your potential wife and/or children from the philosophies, ideas, and values of this world that do not provide healthy food for their minds. Start with the TV and the Internet. What kinds of movies, programs, and other things do you watch? Would you want your wife and children to watch them with you or to do what is being done in what you watch?
8. Protect your potential wife and/or children from the influence of those who would stray and go off on their own or do their own thing even if they call themselves Christians.
9. Protect your potential wife and/or children when they are being criticized or attacked, either by the world or by other Christians.
10. Lead your potential wife and/or children to good, refreshing spiritual food and drink, beginning with God's Word, the Bible. Establish a pattern of daily Scripture reading and prayer with them.
11. Discern the spiritual condition of your potential wife and/or children in order to look out for their welfare.
12. Help your potential wife and children discover God's will for their lives because, in doing his will, they will find rest.
13. Determine your potential wife's and/or children's gifts and capabilities, both natural and spiritual, and develop them accordingly.
14. Discipline your potential wife and/or children with the rod of correction and the staff of the authority that God has given you. Even if they don't like your correction and discipline, do it because it gives them freedom and security. Remember, however, that it is God's authority that you are exercising, so be careful not to abuse it. You will be held accountable to him for how you use it. You are to be a leader, not a dictator.
15. Keep your potential wife and/or children informed. They can help you and support you, even in difficult times, if you share openly with them.

16. Share what you have with your potential wife and/or children when they need it, in abundance, if necessary, and cheerfully.

Additional Scriptural Principles:

Develop a Relationship with God - Love of your potential wife begins with and flows out of your relationship with God. "You shall love the Lord, your God, with all your heart, and with all your soul, and with all your mind. This is the greatest and first commandment." Matthew 22:37 & 38

If you love God, you will "Strive first for the kingdom of God and his righteousness, and all other things will be given to you as well." Matthew 6:33

Love is expressed in faith or trust. "Trust the Lord with all your heart and do not rely on your own insight. In all your ways acknowledge him, and he will make straight your paths." Proverbs 3:5 & 6

"Trust the Lord and do good; so you will live in the land and enjoy security. Take delight in the Lord, and he will give you the desires of your heart. Commit your way to the Lord, trust in him, and he will act." Psalm 37:3-5

Love, faith, trust - these must be the foundations of your relationship with God and then with your potential wife and future children. Remember this! "The Lord is our God, the Lord alone. You shall love the Lord your God with all your heart, and with all your soul, and with all your might. Keep these words. Recite them to your children and talk about them when you are at home and when you are away, when you lie down and when you rise. Bind them as a sign on your hand, fix them as an emblem on your forehead, and write them on the doorposts of your house and on your gates." Deuteronomy 6:4-9

Build Your Home on Peace - Whatever your job or career, your first responsibility and ministry is to your potential wife and family. You commit yourself to this when you get married. "God is a God not of disorder but of peace." 1 Corinthians 14:33 "So, whether you eat or drink, or whatever you do, do everything for the glory of God." 1 Corinthians 10:31

"My people will abide in a peaceful habitation, in secure dwellings, and in quiet resting places." Isaiah 32:18 "Better is a dinner of vegetables where love is than a fatted ox and hatred with it." Proverbs 15:17 If your love for money and possessions becomes stronger than your love and care for your family, there will be hatred and strife instead of love in your family.

Your children will be the result of the love and intimacy between you and your potential wife. Never see them as an accident. God has an essential role in their creation. Through you, he will give them life. "Children are indeed a heritage from the Lord, the fruit of the womb a reward." Psalm 127:3 "Train children in the right way, and when old, they will not stray." Proverbs 22:6

"Fathers, do not provoke your children to anger but bring them up in the discipline and instruction of the Lord." Ephesians 6:4

Do not neglect hospitality, with your potential wife's knowledge, of course. Through it, some have unknowingly entertained angels. Hebrews 13:2

Value Godly Wisdom - Wisdom is the God-given ability to apply knowledge in a practical way. "Wisdom is more precious than jewels, and nothing you desire can compare with her." Proverbs 3:15

"The lips informed by knowledge are a precious jewel." Proverbs 20:15

"By wisdom a home is built, and by understanding it is established; by knowledge the rooms are filled with all precious and pleasant riches." Proverbs 24:3

"If any of you is lacking in wisdom, ask God, who gives to all generously and ungrudgingly, and it will be given you." James 1:5 In fact, you should make it a habit to ask God for wisdom as you begin each day.

Let God Work in and through You - Strive to work in partnership with God. Be aware that you can do nothing worthwhile without him, but that in Christ you can do all things. Paul had the same struggle you do. "We know that the law is spiritual; but I am of the flesh, sold into slavery under sin. I do not understand my own actions. I do not do what I want, but I do the very thing I hate. Now, if I do what I do not want, I agree that the law is good. But, in fact, it is no longer I that do it, but sin that dwells within me. I know nothing good dwells within me, that is, in my flesh. I can will what is right, but I cannot do it. I do not the good I want, but the evil I do not want is what I do. Now, if I do what I do not want, it is no longer I that do it, but sin that dwells within me." Romans 7:14-20

Don't despair, but "work out your own salvation with fear and trembling because it is God who is at work in you, enabling you both to will and to work for his good pleasure." Philippians 2:12 & 13

"For our sake, he (God) made him to be sin who knew no sin (Jesus) so that, in him, we might become the righteousness of God. So, if anyone is in Christ, there is a new creation; everything old has passed away; see, everything has become new!" 2 Corinthians 5:21, 17 You and Christ are an overwhelming majority!

Receive God's Promises to You - "Keep your life free from the love of money but be content with what you have. God has said, 'I will never leave you or forsake you.' " Hebrews 13:5 What a fantastic promise! God has promised to be your provider.

"We know that all things work together for good for those who love God, who are called according to his purpose. Those he foreknew he also predestined to be conformed to the image of his Son in order that he might be the firstborn within a larger family." Romans 8:28 & 29

God is with you even in times of trouble, which are part of life and part of God's plan for you. "We also boast in our sufferings, knowing that suffering produces *endurance*, and endurance produces *character*, and character produces *hope*, and hope does not disappoint us because God's love has been poured out into our hearts through the Holy Spirit that has been given to us." Romans 5:3-5 "No testing has overtaken you that is not common to everyone. God is faithful, and he will not let you be tested beyond your strength, but with the testing he will also provide the way out so that you may be able to endure it." Corinthians 10:13 Therefore, "cast all your anxiety upon him because he cares for you." 1 Peter 5:7

Accept Your Potential Wife the Way She Is - Don't try to change her. Let God do it through your prayers and the example of your love. "Let the same mind be in you that you have in Christ Jesus, who, though he was in the form of God, did not regard equality with God as something to be exploited, but emptied himself, taking the form of a slave, being born in human likeness. And, being found in human form, he humbled himself and became obedient to the point of death - even death on a cross." Philippians 2:5-8 As you submit to Christ over you, your wife will submit to your authority over her.

"Each of you should love his wife as himself, and a wife should respect her husband." Ephesians 5:33. You must understand this: let everyone be quick to listen, slow to speak, slow to anger; for you anger does not produce God's righteousness." James 1:19 Love your wife, be quick to listen to her rather than to talk at her. Then, watch the changes take place!

Be Content with Where God Has You - A loving parent will not give in to a child when it throws a tantrum. Neither will God! "I have learned to be content with whatever I have. I know what it is to have little, and I know what it is to have plenty. In any and all circumstances, I have learned the secret of being well-fed and of going hungry, of having plenty and of being in need. I can do all things through him who strengthens me." Philippians 4:11b-13 Like Paul, you must learn to be satisfied where you *are* so that God is free to move you to a *better* place. Let *God* move you in his time and in his way. Therefore, "give thanks in all circumstances, for this is the will of God in Christ Jesus for you." 1 Thessalonians 5:18.

Admit Your Constant Need for Forgiveness - You cannot hide anything from God. He knows everything about you because he made you. Learn, then, that "no one who conceals transgressions will prosper, but one who confesses and forsakes them will obtain mercy." Proverbs 28:13

"If we confess our sins, he who is faithful and just will forgive us our sins and cleanse us from all unrighteousness." 1 John 1:9

"You have held back my life from the pit of destruction, for you have cast all my sins behind your back." Isaiah 38: 17b

God says to you, "I, I am he who blots out your transgressions for my own sake, and I will not remember your sins." Isaiah 43:25 "I will be merciful toward their iniquities, and I will remember their sins no more." Hebrews 8:12

YOUR POSITION AS A POTENTIAL HUSBAND-FATHER

I. God's Authority Line - Authority is the *right* to say or do something. Power is the ability to get things done or to keep them from being done. Your authority as a potential husband-father is God-given, and you will answer to him for how you use it. Your power to be a good husband-father also comes from God the Father through Jesus Christ and in the power of the Holy Spirit.

God the Father is the head of Christ, Christ is the head of every man, and the husband is the head of his wife and children, if any. 1 Corinthians 11:3

II. Foundation Principles - To be a godly husband-father, you need to develop a personal relationship with God the Father and to learn how he acts as a Father to us, his children. "In the fear of the Lord, one has strong confidence, and one's children will have a refuge." "Happy is everyone who fears the Lord, who walks in his ways. You will eat the fruit of the labor of your hands; you will be happy, and it will go well with you. Your wife will be like a fruitful vine within your house; your children will be like olive shoots around your table. Thus will the man be blessed who fears the Lord." Proverbs 14:26; Psalms 128:1-4

It is important to establish healthy financial priorities. You will need to live within the means *your* job provides, not your potential wife's, unless circumstances and the Lord's will determine otherwise. If you get into a situation where your potential wife *has* to work to make house payments or to meet other financial debts, you will be in a *trap*. You will need to work your way out of this situation as quickly as possible and set her free. Work that is not done *freely* is slavery and bondage. She will need to have the freedom to choose to *work* for her own satisfaction or fulfillment or to *stay home*. "Prepare your work outside, get everything ready for you in the field, and, after that, build your house." Proverbs 25:27

God will not honor dishonesty in your job or in your business. "Those who are greedy for unjust gain make trouble for their households. Those who trouble their households will inherit wind, and the fool will be servant to the wise." Proverbs 15:27; 11:29

Establish in your spirit that God is your sole *Source* for your total provision and let him determine the *means*. Ordinarily, this is your job. It is not the lottery or other questionable sources. Trust him for your finances and then manage them wisely. Also, don't let your own *wants* for material things come before your potential family's *needs*. It can destroy you. "The house of the wicked is destroyed, but the tent of the upright flourishes." "The Lord tears down the house of the proud." Proverbs 14:11; Proverbs 15:25a

III. Proper Attitudes toward Your Wife - You are to provide loving protection and guidance for your potential wife. Don't be afraid to correct her when appropriate, but do so in love and with gentleness. Watch your own motives. She is to be your helpmate not your doormat or your slave. "Happy is the husband of a good wife; the number of his days will be doubled. A loyal wife brings joy to her husband, and he will complete his years in peace. A good wife is a great blessing; she will be granted among the blessings of the man who fears the Lord. Whether rich or poor, his heart is content, and at all times his face is cheerful." Sirach 26:1-4

Yes, "he who finds a wife finds a good thing, and obtains favor from the Lord." "House and wealth are inherited from parents, but a prudent wife is from the Lord." "He who acquires a wife gets his best possession, a helper fit for him and a pillar of support." "A friend or companion is always welcome, but a sensible wife is better than either." Proverbs 18:22; 19:14; Sirach 36:29; 40:23

"Each of you should know how to control your own body in holiness and honor, not with lustful passion, like the unbelievers who do not know God." "Husbands, in the same way, show consideration for your wives in your lives together, paying honor to the woman as the weaker sex since they are also heirs of the gracious gift of life, so that nothing may hinder your prayers" 1 Thessalonians 4:4 & 5; 1 Peter 3:7.

"Do not be jealous of the wife of your bosom or you will teach her an evil lesson to your own hurt. Do not give yourself to a woman and let her trample down your strength. Do not go near a loose woman, or you will fall into her snares." "Drink water from your own cistern, flowing water from your own well." "Let your fountain be yours alone, not one shared with strangers; and, have joy of the wife of your youth, your lovely hind, your graceful doe. Her love will invigorate you always; through her love you will flourish continually." "Husbands, love your wives and never treat them harshly." "Love your wives, just as Christ loved the Church and gave himself up for her." Sirach 9:1-3; Proverbs 5:15; Proverbs 5:17-19 New American Bible; Colossians 3:19; Ephesians 5:25

IV. Proper Attitudes toward Your Children - It will be primarily your responsibility to love, nurture, and discipline your potential children. They will be watching and learning from you as their primary leader and teacher. They will first learn to love or to hate God the Father based on how you treat them. They will follow where you lead - for good or for bad. "The righteous walk in integrity -- happy are the children who follow them!" "Do not desire a multitude of worthless children, and do not rejoice in ungodly offspring. If they multiply, do not rejoice in them unless the fear of the Lord is in them. Do not trust in their survival or rely on their numbers; for one can be better than a thousand, and to die childless better than to have ungodly children." Proverbs 20:7; Sirach 16:1-3

20 Principles of a Father's Relationship with His Children
Lowell Davey, President of BBN

1. You must establish boundaries.
2. You must enjoy your children.
3. You must eliminate evil influences.
4. You must expose your humanity as their parent.
5. You must explain your reasons whenever possible.
6. You must exchange ideas with your children.
7. You must encourage your children daily.
8. You must elevate their gifts.
9. You must instruct them in the way to go.
10. You must expand their horizons.
11. You must express physical attention.
12. You must examine their distinct personalities.
13. You must extend patience to them.
14. You must enter into their victories and defeats
15. You must ever be ready to communicate.
16. You must evaluate your children's decisions.
17. You must exonerate each other as husband and wife.
18. You must examine your own life as an example.
19. You must expose them daily to the Word of God.

20. You must exemplify Jesus Christ in your personal life.

V. Basic Goals for Christian Husbands and Fathers - As a Christian potential husband and father, you should seek to be above reproach; the husband of one wife, whose children are believers, not accused of debauchery and not rebellious; temperate; sensible; respectable; hospitable; a lover of goodness; prudent; upright; devout; self-controlled; an apt teacher who has a firm grasp of the word that is trustworthy in accordance with the teachings so that you may be able both to preach with sound doctrine and to refute those who contradict it; not a drunkard or addicted to wine; not violent but gentle; not quarrelsome; and not a lover of money or greedy for gain. You must manage your own household well, keeping your children submissive and respectful in every way; for, if you do not know how to manage your own household, how can you take care of God's Church? Moreover, you must be well thought of by outsiders so that you may not fall into disgrace and the snare of the devil. 1 Timothy 3:2-5, 7; Titus 1:6-9

FATHER: Prophet - Priest - King

PROPHET - To Guide: Listens to the Lord and ministers to his family what God is saying to his family.

PRIEST - To Guard: As the priest listened to the congregation and took their request to the Lord, the Father is to spend time with his family to know their need and then to take those needs before the Lord.

KING - To Govern: Not to be as an earthly king who lords it over his people but to be a heavenly king who is a servant to his family.

Family Foundations International, PO Box 320, Littleton, CO 80160

PRAYER OF CONSECRATION AND DEDICATION OF YOUR HOME

Father, as the prophet, priest, and king of this home, I dedicate and consecrate it to the Lord Jesus Christ. I declare that Satan has no hold on it. I surrender everything in this house, and every room in it, to the Lordship of Jesus Christ and place it under his protection.

In the Name of Jesus Christ, I bind and cast out every evil spirit that may be in this house. I command them to leave and go to the driest places and the deepest oceans.

I claim by faith that everything in this house is covered under the Blood of Jesus, from the top of the roof to the bottom of the footings and everything in between. I claim by faith that this house is surrounded by a hedge of thorns, a wall of fire, and a wall of faith. I pray that warring angels would come to protect the four corners of this house and everyone inside.

Father, I ask you to bless and use this house for your glory so that through it, and through us, people may be brought to perfection as one, that they may know that you sent Jesus and that you love them as you love us. I ask this in the name of the Father, and the Son, and the Holy Spirit. Thank you, Father, for the complete victory we already have in Jesus Christ. Amen.

THE RULE OF ST. BENEDICT FOR MODERN FATHERS

1. Treat each person in the family according to his or her particular needs. Christian equality doesn't mean we all get the same thing; it means we all get what we need. You must adapt and fit yourself to all: one needs to be encouraged, another to be rebuked, another to be persuaded, each one according to his or her own nature. One child may need gentle encouragement, another may need a tough regime.

2. Show the tough attitude of the master and also the loving affection of a father. You must balance the toughness of a drill sergeant with the tenderness of a nurse. A wise father combines the strengths of both characters while leaving the faults behind.

3. You must lead by your actions as much as by your teaching. It is an awesome thought that, in the long run, children will do as we do, not as we say. You also must live according to the rule of Christ and must be seen to obey the principles you put forward for others.

4. Create in your family a constant spirit of forgiveness. Train your children to come to you instantly to ask forgiveness and then forgive at the first request. Do not let the sun go down on anger, yours or other's. In a Christian home, you cannot ignore conflict and hope problems will go away. The Christian dad has the responsibility to wade in, solve the problem, and insist on mutual and real forgiveness.

5. Teach the important principle of obedience. The word obedience has its root in "to listen." Listen to God and to one another. This sensitive listening and awareness of the needs of others lies at the heart of a peaceful family. Obey one another in love. An attitude of mutual service and attention to one another will help build good communication as well as confidence and natural good manners.

6. Bad behavior means that a family member doesn't know how to act in community. Physical punishment is not always effective. He or she should be excluded from the family community. Separating a child from a special treat or from the family activity is usually punishment enough. Even this punishment must be done with compassion and a deep concern for the offender's welfare and never in rage or a desire for revenge. In a spirit of conciliation and concern, you might ask the child's mother or a brother or a sister to go and cheer him or her up.

7. The Christian family must be a community of prayer. Prayer must be natural and from the heart. "Indeed, we must grasp that it is not by using many words that we shall get our prayers answered but by purity of heart...Prayer therefore should be short and pure." Prayer is better short, sharp, and sincere, not long-winded and showy.

St. Benedict's practical principles root you firmly in your present situation. He believes that God is to be found here and now, not there and then. He is found in the face of your wife and children. He is found in the terrible moments of family life as well as in the wonderful ones. These principles will help you to cope with reality as you live it day by day.

--adapted from an article by Dwight Longenecker, author of *Listen My Son,* (Morehouse Publishing), a commentary on the Rule of St. Benedict for fathers.

PERSONAL EVALUATION FOR POTENTIAL HUSBANDS

1. So deeply do I care for you, my family, that I am determined to share with you not only the Gospel of God but also my own self because you have become very dear to me. You remember my labor and toil. I work night and day so that I might not burden you. You are witnesses, and God also, how pure, upright, and blameless my conduct is toward you. As you know, I deal with each one of you, urging and encouraging you and pleading that you lead a life worthy of God, who calls you into his kingdom and glory. 1 Thessalonians 1:8-12

    Does this Scripture describe my attitude and commitment toward my own family?

    YES ( )   NO ( )   SOMETIMES ( )

2. Husbands, love your wives and never treat them harshly. Fathers, do not provoke your children, or they may lose heart. Colossians 3:19, 21

    Is there hidden bitterness and resentment in my heart that I need to deal with?

    YES ( )   NO ( )   I DIDN'T KNOW THERE WAS ( )

3. Those conflicts and disputes among you, where do they come from? Do they not come from your cravings that are at war within you? By insolence, the heedless make strife, but wisdom is with those who take advice. James 4:1; Proverbs 13:10

    Do (Did) I find it difficult to control my temper during conflicts with my own family?

    YES ( )   NO ( )   SOMETIMES ( )   TOO OFTEN ( )

4. Confess your sins to one another and pray for one another so that you may be healed. Leave your gift before the altar and go; first, be reconciled to your brother or sister, and then come and offer your gift. James 5:16; Matthew 5:24

    Do (Did) I make it a practice to verbally acknowledge to my own family when I have been wrong?

    YES ( )   NO ( )   SOMETIMES ( )

5. We are God's servants, working together; you are God's field, God's building. According to the grace of God given to me, like a skilled master builder I laid a foundation. 1 Corinthians 3:9

    Do I have clearly defined standards and ideals of character development for myself and for my future family?

    YES ( )   NO ( )   I HADN'T THOUGHT ABOUT IT ( )

6. Be doers of the word and not merely hearers who deceive themselves. James 1:22

> Do (Did) I encourage and help my own family
> achieve these standards rather than criticize
> them when they fall (fell) short?
>
> YES ( )   NO ( )   NOT LIKE I SHOULD ( )

7. Fathers, do not provoke your children to anger but bring them up in the discipline and instruction of the Lord. Ephesians 6:4

> Have I helped each member of my own family
> set up clearly defined standards to develop
> inward qualities and outward achievement?
>
> YES ( )   NO ( )   I HADN'T THOUGHT ABOUT IT ( )

8. Do your best to present yourself to God as one approved by him, a worker who has no need to be ashamed, rightly explaining the word of truth. Avoid profane chatter because it will lead people into more and more impiety, and their talk will spread like gangrene. 2 Timothy 2:15-17

> Does my language and conversation indicate
> to others that I am a Christian?
>
> YES ( )   NO ( )   IT SURE DOESN'T ( )

9. If any of you is lacking in wisdom, ask God, who gives to all generously and ungrudgingly, and it will be given to you. James 1:5

> Do I ask for wisdom every day to guide me?
>
> YES ( )   NO ( )   I NEVER THOUGHT ABOUT IT ( )

10. If your brother or sister sins, go and point out the fault when the two of you are alone. If he or she listens to you, you have regained that one. But, if you are not listened to, take one or two others along with you so that every word may be confirmed by the evidence of two or three witnesses. Matthew 18:15 & 16

> Do I believe that I know how to apply basic Scriptural
> principles to achieving lasting solutions for family conflicts?
>
> YES ( )   NO ( )   I NEED HELP ( )

11. Husbands, love your wives, just as Christ loved the Church and gave himself up for her. For, the husband is head of the wife just as Christ is Head of the Church, the Body of which he is the Savior. Ephesians 5:25, 23

> Have I clearly defined my role in the home?
>
> YES ( )   NO ( )   I NEVER UNDERSTOOD MY ROLE ( )

12. Christ Jesus came into the world to save sinners. But, for that very reason, I received mercy

so that, in me, Jesus Christ might display the utmost patience, making me an example to those who would come to believe in him for eternal life. 1 Timothy 1:15b & 16

> My future family's attitude toward my authority will tend to become their attitude toward God's authority. Am I satisfied with what their response might be to my example and my authority?

YES ( )   NO ( )   I NEED SOME IMPROVEMENT ( )

13. Husbands, love your wives, just as Christ loved the Church and gave himself up for her in order to make her holy by cleansing her with the washing of water by the Word so as to present the Church to himself in splendor, without a spot or wrinkle or anything of the kind, yes, so that she may be holy and without blemish. In the same way, husbands should love their wives as they do their own bodies. He who loves his wife loves himself. For, no one ever hates his own body, but he nourishes and tenderly cares for it, just as Christ does for the Church, because we are members of his Body. Ephesians 5:25-30

> Would my potential wife and family respect me to the same degree that Jesus Christ is to be respected by the Church?

YES ( )   NO ( )   I'M AFRAID NOT ( )

14. Pleasant words are like a honeycomb, sweetness to the soul and health to the body. Proverbs 16:24.

> Do (Did) I notice and compliment my own family for things done around the house? Do (Did) I give personal compliments?

YES ( )   NO ( )   NOT OFTEN ENOUGH ( )

15. Do you see someone who is hasty in speech? There is more hope for a fool than for anyone like that. One who spares words is knowledgeable; one who is cool in spirit has understanding. Even fools who keep silent are considered wise; when they close their lips, they are deemed intelligent. Proverbs 29:20; 17:27 & 28

> Do (Did) I degrade my own family members in front of one another or, worse yet, in front of others?

YES ( )   NO ( )   MUCH TOO OFTEN ( )

16. Know well the condition of your flocks and give attention to your herds. Proverbs 27:23.

> Do (Did) I discuss family problems and seek Scriptural solutions together with my own family?

YES ( )   NO ( )   I HADN'T THOUGHT ABOUT IT ( )

17. Just as water reflects the face, so one human heart reflects another. The purposes in the human mind are like deep water, but the intelligent will draw them out. Proverbs 27:19; 20:5

> Do I initiate discussions with my own family regarding their areas of interest or their activities in church, school, and so forth?
>
> YES ( )   NO ( )   NOT VERY OFTEN ( )

18. Fathers, do not provoke your children to anger but bring them up in the discipline and instruction of the Lord. Ephesians 6:4

> Do (Did) I pray with and for my own family as well as my potential wife?
>
> YES ( )   NO ( )   NOT VERY OFTEN ( )

19. The clever see danger and hide, but the simple go on and suffer for it. I say to you that everyone who looks at a woman with lust has already committed adultery with her in his heart. Proverbs 22:3; Matthew 5:28

> Do I flirt with or over-compliment women?
> Am I overly conscious of women?
>
> YES ( )   NO ( )   MORE THAN I WAS AWARE OF ( )

20. Give instruction to the wise, and they will become wiser still. Teach the righteous, and they will gain in learning. By insolence, the heedless make strife, but wisdom is with those who take advice. The good leave an inheritance to their children's children, but the sinner's wealth is laid up for the righteous. Fathers, do not provoke your children to anger but bring them up in the discipline and instruction of the Lord. Proverbs 9:9; 13:10, 22; Ephesians 6:4

> Do I seem to spend my time giving orders instead of providing instruction?
>
> YES ( )   NO ( )   MUCH TOO OFTEN ( )

21. I walk in the way of righteousness, along the paths of justice, endowing with wealth those who love me and filling their treasuries. Proverbs 8:20 & 21

> Do (Did) I spend time alone with each of my own family members?
>
> YES ( )   NO ( )   NOT NEARLY ENOUGH ( )

22. Incline your ear and hear my words and apply your mind to my teaching; for, it will be pleasant if you keep them within you, if all of them are ready on your lips. So that your trust may be in the Lord, I have made them known to you today, yes, to you. Have I not written for you sayings of admonition and knowledge, to show you what is right and true so that you may

give a true answer to those who sent you? Proverbs 22:17-21

> Is (Was) my testimony at home one that I would be willing to share with anyone?
>
> YES ( )   NO ( )   NOT AT THE PRESENT TIME ( )

23. Husbands, love your wives, just as Christ loved the Church and gave himself up for her. Ephesians 5:25

> Could observers, from the quality and degree of love that I show for my own family, learn anything at all about the greatness of God's love for them?
>
> YES ( )   NO ( )   I'M AFRAID NOT ( )

24. Read the Song of Solomon, also called the Song of Songs.

> Do I have a Scriptural concept of the role of sex in marriage, that it is intended by God to provide pleasure and fun for both the husband and the wife?
>
> YES ( )   NO ( )   I NEVER THOUGHT OF IT THAT WAY ( )

Read the following.

CHURCH TEACHING ON THE SANCTITY OF LIFE

"Human life is sacred because, from its beginning, it involves the creative action of God and it remains forever in a special relationship with the Creator, who is its sole end. God alone is the Lord of life from its beginning until its end. No one can, under any circumstance, claim for oneself the right directly to destroy an innocent human being." (*The Gift of Life*, Introduction, 5)

Of all visible creatures, only human beings are able to know and love their creator. They are the only creatures on earth that God has willed for their own sake. They alone are called to share, by knowledge and love, in God's own life. It was for this end that they were created, and this is the fundamental reason for their dignity.

The covenant between God and mankind is interwoven with reminders of God's gift of human life and man's murderous violence: "For your lifeblood, I will surely require a reckoning….Whoever sheds the blood of people, by people shall that one's blood be shed for God made people in his own image" (Genesis 9:5 & 6). The Old Testament always considered blood a sacred sign of life (cf. Leviticus 17:14). This teaching remains necessary for all time.

Scripture specifies the prohibition contained in the fifth commandment: "Do not slay the innocent and the righteous" (Exodus 23:7). The deliberate murder of an innocent person is gravely contrary to the dignity of the human being, to the golden rule, and to the holiness of the Creator. The law forbidding it is universally valid. It obliges each and every one, always and everywhere.

The natural law, present in the heart of each person and established by reason, is universal in its precepts, and its authority extends to all people. It expresses the dignity of the person and determines the basis for one's fundamental rights and duties. The great Roman Orator, Cicero, put it this way: "For there is at true law: right reason. It is in conformity with nature, is diffused among all people, and is immutable and eternal. Its orders summon to duty, its prohibitions turn away from offense….To replace it with a contrary law is a sacrilege. Failure to apply even one of its provisions is forbidden. No one can abrogate it entirely." (Cicero, *Republic III, 22, 33*)

In the Sermon on the Mount, the Lord recalls the commandment, "You shall not kill" (Matthew 5:21) and adds to it the proscription of anger, hatred, and vengeance. Going further, Christ asks his disciples to turn the other cheek, to love their enemies (cf. Matthew 5:22-39; 5:44). He did not defend himself and told Peter to leave his sword in its sheath (Matthew 26:52).

Christian prayer extends to the *forgiveness of enemies* (Matthew 5:43 & 44), transfiguring the disciple by configuring one to one's Master. Forgiveness is a high point of Christian prayer. Only hearts attuned to God's compassion can receive the gift of prayer. Forgiveness also bears witness that, in our world, love is stronger than sin. Forgiveness is the fundamental condition of the reconciliation of the children of God with their Father and of people with one another.

Legitimate Defense

The legitimate defense of persons and societies is not an exception to the prohibition against the murder of the innocent that constitutes intentional killing. The act of self-defense can have a double effect: the preservation of one's own life and the killing of the aggressor. The one is intended, the other is not (St. Thomas Acquinas, *STh II-II, 64, corp. art.*). An effect can be tolerated without being willed by its agent, for instance, a mother's exhaustion from tending her sick child. A bad effect is not imputable if it was not willed either as an end or as a means of an action, e.g., a death a person incurs in aiding someone in danger. For a bad effect to be imputable, it must be foreseeable, and the agent must have the possibility of avoiding it, as in the case of manslaughter caused by a drunken driver.

Love toward oneself remains a fundamental principle of morality. Therefore, it is legitimate to insist on respect for one's own right to life. Someone who defends one's life is not guilty of murder even if one is forced to deal his aggressor a lethal blow.

Legitimate defense can be not only a right but also a grave duty for someone responsible for another's life, the common good of the family or of the state. Submission to authority and co-responsibility for the common good make it morally obligatory to defend one's country. Preserving the common good of society requires rendering the aggressor unable to inflict harm. For this reason, the traditional teaching of the Church has acknowledged as well-founded the right and duty of legitimate public authority to punish malefactors by means of penalties commensurate with the gravity of the crime, not excluding, in cases of extreme gravity, the death penalty. For analogous reasons, those holding authority have the right to repel by armed force aggressors against the community in their charge.

"Human society can be neither well-ordered nor prosperous unless it has some people invested with legitimate authority to preserve its institutions and to devote themselves as far as is necessary to work and care for the good of all" (Pope St. John XXIII). By "authority" one means the quality by virtue of which persons or institutions make laws and give orders to people and expect obedience from them. Every human community needs an authority to govern it. The foundation of such authority lies in human nature. It is necessary for the unity of the state. Its role is to ensure as far as possible the common good of the society.

If bloodless means are sufficient to defend human lives against an aggressor and to protect public order and the safety of persons, public authority should limit itself to such means because they better correspond to the concrete conditions of the common good and are more in conformity to the dignity of the human person.

Intentional Homicide

The fifth commandment forbids *direct and intentional killing* as gravely sinful. The murderer and those who cooperate voluntarily in murder commit a sin that cries out to Heaven for vengeance. Infanticide, fratricide, patricide, and the murder of a spouse are especially grave crimes by reason of the natural bonds that they break. Concern for eugenics or public health cannot justify any murder, even if commanded by public authority.

The fifth commandment forbids doing anything with the intention of *indirectly* bringing about a person's death. The moral law prohibits exposing someone to mortal danger without grave reason, as well as refusing assistance to a person in danger. The acceptance by human society of murderous famines, without efforts to remedy them, is a scandalous injustice and a grave offense. Those whose usurious and avaricious dealings lead to the hunger and death of their brethren in the human family indirectly commit homicide, which is imputable to them (cf. Amos 8-4-10).

Unintentional killing is not morally imputable. But, one is not exonerated from grave offense if, without proportionate reasons, one has acted in a way that brings about someone's death, even without the intention to do so. The virtue of temperance disposes us to *avoid every kind of excess*: the abuse of food, alcohol, tobacco, or medicine. Those incur grave guilt who, by drunkenness or a love of speed, endanger their own and others' safety on the road, at sea, or in the air. Temperance is the moral virtue that moderates the attraction of pleasures and provides balance in the use of created goods. It ensures the will's mastery over instincts and keeps desires within the limits of what is honorable. The temperate person directs the sensitive appetites toward what is good and maintains a healthy discretion.

Abortion

Human life must be respected and protected absolutely from the moment of conception. From the first moment of his or her existence, a human being must be recognized as having the rights of a person - among which is the inviolable right of every innocent being to life (*The Gift of Life* I, I). Endowed with a spiritual and immortal soul, the human person is the only person on earth that God has willed for its own sake. From his or her conception, he or she is destined for eternal beatitude.

"Before I formed you in the womb, I knew you; and before you were born, I consecrated you" (Jeremiah 1:5; cf. Job 10:8-12; Psalm 22:10 & 11). "My frame was not hidden from you, when I was being made in secret, intricately wrought in the depths of the earth" (Psalm 139:15).

Since the first century, the Church has affirmed the moral evil of every procured abortion. This teaching has not changed and remains unchangeable. Direct abortion, that is to say, abortion willed either as an end or a means, is gravely contrary to the moral law.

"You shall not kill the embryo by abortion and shall not cause the newborn to perish" (*Didache* 2,2). "For us, murder is once and for all forbidden; so even the child in the womb, while yet the mother's blood is still being drawn on to form the human being, it is not lawful for us to destroy. To forbid birth is only to murder the sooner. It makes no difference whether one takes away the life once born or destroys it as it comes to birth. He is a man who is to be a man; the fruit is always present in the seed" (Tertullian c 220, *Apology,* 9:8)

God, the author of life, has entrusted to human beings the noble mission of safeguarding life, and people must carry it out in a manner worthy of themselves. Life must be protected with the utmost care from the moment of conception: abortion and infanticide are abominable crimes.

Formal cooperation in an abortion constitutes a grave offense. The Church attaches the canonical penalty of excommunication to this crime against human life. The Church does not, thereby, intend to restrict the scope of mercy. Rather, she makes clear the gravity of the crime committed, the irreparable harm done to the innocent who is put to death, as well as to the parents and the whole society.

The inalienable right to life of every innocent human individual is a *constitutive element of a civil society and its legislation:* "The inalienable rights of the person must be recognized and respected by civil society and the political authority. These human rights depend neither on single individuals nor on parents; nor do they represent a concession made by society and the State. They belong to human nature and are inherent in a person by virtue of the creative act from which the person took one's origin.

Among such fundamental rights, one should mention in this regard every human being's right to life and physical integrity from the moment of conception until death. "The moment a positive law deprives a category of human beings of the protection that civil legislation ought to accord them, the State is denying the equality of all before the law. When the State does not place its power at the service of the rights of each citizen, and in particular of the more vulnerable, the very foundations of a State based on law are undermined....As a consequence of the respect and protection that must be ensured for the unborn child from the moment of conception, the law must provide appropriate penal sanctions for every deliberate violation of the child's rights" (*The Gift of Life* III).

Since it must be treated from conception as a person, the embryo must be defended in its integrity, cared for, and healed, as far as possible, like any other human being. "*Prenatal diagnosis* is morally licit, 'if it respects the life and integrity of the embryo and the human fetus and is directed toward its safeguarding or healing as an individual....It is gravely opposed to the moral law when this is done with the thought of possibly inducing an abortion, depending upon the results: a diagnosis must not be the equivalent of a death sentence' " (*The Gift of Life* I, 2).

"One must hold as licit procedures carried out on the human embryo that respect the life and integrity of the embryo, do not involve disproportionate risk for it, and are directed toward its healing, the improvement of its condition of health or its individual survival" (*The Gift of Life* I, 3). "It is immoral to produce human embryos intended for exploitation as disposable biological material" (*The Gift of Life* I, 5). "Certain attempts to *influence chromosomic or genetic inheritance* are not therapeutic but are aimed at producing human beings selected according to sex or other predetermined qualities. Such manipulations are contrary to the personal dignity of the human being and one's integrity and identity that are unique and unrepeatable" (*The Gift of Life* I, 6).

Euthanasia Or "Mercy Killing"

Those whose lives are diminished or weakened deserve special respect. Sick or handicapped persons should be helped to lead lives as normal as possible. Christ's compassion toward the sick and his many healings of every kind of infirmity are a resplendent sign that "God has visited his people" (Luke 7:16; cf. Matthew 4:24) and that the kingdom of God is close at hand. Jesus has the power not only to heal but also to forgive sins (cf. Mark 2:5-12). He has come to heal the whole person, soul and body. He is the physician the sick have need of (cf. Mark 2:17). His compassion toward all who suffer goes so far that he identifies himself with them: "I was sick and you visited me" (Matthew 25:36). His preferential love for the sick has not ceased through the centuries to draw the very special attention of Christians toward all those who suffer in body and soul. It is the source of tireless efforts to comfort them.

Whatever its motives and means, direct euthanasia consists in putting an end to the life of handicapped, sick or dying persons. It is morally unacceptable. Thus, an act or omission that, of itself or by intention, causes death in order to eliminate suffering constitutes a murder gravely contrary to the dignity of the human person and to the respect due to the living God, one's Creator. The error of judgment into which one can fall in good faith does not change the nature of this murderous act that must always be forbidden and excluded.

Discontinuing medical procedures that are burdensome, dangerous, extraordinary, or disproportionate to the expected outcome can be legitimate. It is the refusal of "over-zealous" treatment. Here, one does not will to cause death, but one's inability to impede it is merely accepted. The decisions should be made by the patient if one is competent and able or, if not, by those legally entitled to act for the patient, whose reasonable will and legitimate interests must always be respected.

Even if death is thought imminent, the ordinary care owed to a sick person cannot be legitimately interrupted. The use of painkillers to alleviate the sufferings of the dying, even at the risk of shortening their days, can be morally in conformity with human dignity if death is not willed as either an end or a means but only foreseen and tolerated as inevitable. Palliative care is a special form of disinterested charity. As such, it should be encouraged.

Suicide

Everyone is responsible for one's life before God, who has given it. It is God who remains the sovereign Master of life. We are obliged to accept life gratefully and preserve it for his honor and the salvation of our souls. We are stewards, not owners, of the life God has entrusted to us. It is not ours to dispose of.

Suicide contradicts the natural inclination of the human being to preserve and perpetuate one's life. It is gravely contrary to the just love of self. It likewise offends love of neighbor because it unjustly breaks the ties of solidarity with family, nation, and other human societies to which we continue to have obligations. Suicide is contrary to love for the living God.

The fourth commandment *illuminates other relationships in society.* In our brothers and sisters, we see the children of our parents; in our cousins, the descendents of our ancestors; in our fellow citizens, the children of our country; in the baptized, the children of our mother the Church; in every human person, a son or daughter of the One who wants to be called "our Father." In this way, our relationships with our neighbors are recognized as personal in character. The neighbor is not a "unit" in the human collective but is "someone" who by one's known origins deserves particular attention and respect.

If suicide is committed with the intention of setting an example, especially to the young, it also takes on the gravity of scandal. Scandal is an attitude or behavior that leads another to do evil.

The person who gives scandal becomes one's neighbor's tempter. One damages virtue and integrity and may even draw one's brother or sister into spiritual death. Scandal is a grave offense if, by deed or omission, another is deliberately led into a grave offense. Anyone who uses the power at one's disposal in such a way that it leads others to do wrong becomes guilty of scandal and responsible for the evil that one has directly or indirectly encouraged. Voluntary cooperation in suicide is also contrary to the moral law.

Imputability and responsibility for an action can be diminished or even nullified by ignorance, inadvertence, duress, fear, habit, inordinate attachments, and other psychological or social factors. Grave psychological disturbances, anguish, or grave fear of hardship, suffering, or torture can diminish the responsibility of the one committing suicide. Thus, we should not despair of the eternal salvation of persons who have taken their own lives. By ways know to one alone, God can provide the opportunity for salutary repentance. For this reason, the Church prays for persons who have taken their own lives.

--compiled by Patrick J. Hession from *Catechism of the Catholic Church*

ABORTION, IN VETRO FERTILIZATION, AND OTHER ABERRATIONS

A young woman trashes her newborn child.
People condemn her and call it murder.

A woman trashes her unborn child.
People applaud her and call it abortion.

--Patrick J. Hession

Introduction

Birth control, contraception, sterilization, abortion, and euthanasia are as old as mankind. The first methods of contraception were recorded in Egypt 1800 years before Christ. Abortion was condemned 2000 years before Christ. With the coming of Christ, contraception was opposed from the beginning, appearing in non-biblical Christian writings as early as 70. It was not until 1930 that the first break came in the acceptance of contraceptives as a means of birth control. In 1930, the bishops of the Anglican Church stated that the use of contraceptives was morally acceptable in very extreme cases, but hopefully abstinence would be used.

A July 1989 Gallup Poll showed that 29% of Americans wanted to keep abortion legal in all circumstance, 17% would make abortion illegal for all reasons, 51% would restrict abortion to very limited circumstances. A *Boston Globe* poll of March 1989 found that only 25% of Americans would keep abortion legal in all circumstances, 19% would make abortion illegal for all reasons, 53% would limit abortion to the small percentage of cases involving rape, incest, the life or physical health of the mother, or genetic fetal deformity.

A myth perpetrated by pro-abortion groups is that, with restrictions on access to legal abortion, many women would die from illegal or unsafe abortions, and that 10,000 a year died that way before the 1973 *Roe vs. Wade* decision of the Supreme Court. The reality is that, before 1973, fewer than 100 women died annually from abortion. The national Centers for Disease Control put the total abortion deaths in 1972 at 83.

Margaret Sanger founded Planned Parenthood, the major perpetrator of all of these aberrations today.

She was born in New York, married three times, and had many lovers. In 1915, she was jailed for propagating contraception. In 1920, she founded the Birth Control League of America, but because this name had a negative connotation, it was later changed to Planned Parenthood.

Margaret Sanger was a firm believer in eugenics, a science that deals with selective breeding and genetic engineering to produce a superior race. Her friends were socialists and anarchists, and she conferred with Hitler's chief of staff on eugenics. Her magazines and journals were filled with writings and articles by well-known eugenicists and members of Hitler's Third Reich. In her travels, she counseled Ghandi that the means of economic stability was through birth control. Ghandi's response was, "The only birth control worthy of humans was self-control." Margaret Sanger died at the age of 87, an alcoholic and drug addict. Each year, Planned Parenthood gives the "Margaret Sanger Award."

The public deserves to know the facts about Planned Parenthood. The national organization is among the leading abortion providers, performing across the nation 264,943 abortion procedures in 2005 alone, a 29 percent increase since 2000. Teens and young people are the primary customers for their services and information, which include the distribution of contraception, emergency contraception, and chemical and surgical abortions. Nationally, 70 percent of Planned Parenthood's customers are under age 25 and 27 percent are under age 19. Furthermore, Planned Parenthood is a supplier of graphic and explicit sex educational materials. These materials are being used in public schools.

Planned Parenthood calls itself pro-child, pro-woman, and pro-family. Yet, it is an organization based on falsehoods about the human person, the family, and community life. When a minor comes to Planned Parenthood, she is provided information on contraception, sex education, and treatment of STDs without parental notification. How can Planned Parenthood justify calling itself pro-family or pro-child, when it intrudes itself between a child and parent?

Planned Parenthood vigorously opposes any legislation that would provide advance medical information pertaining to an abortion procedure, any legislation that would provide a woman who is seeking an abortion knowledge of her unborn child's development, or information regarding alternatives to abortion. Considering the psychological and physical effects of abortion on a woman, how can Planned Parenthood call itself pro-woman and oppose widespread access to advanced information?

Until 1963, Planned Parenthood published a pamphlet that contained the question: "Is contraception like abortion?" The answer: "No. Contraception prevents ovum and sperm from meeting. Abortion kills the life of a baby after it has begun. It is dangerous to your life and health." One theory given for Planned Parenthood's change in viewpoint is that Rockefeller refused further financial support unless the group embraced abortion. Planned Parenthood operates over 50 abortion centers in the United States and is the single greatest killer of babies in the world. In most counties, it is funded through the United Way.

In 1918, when Margaret Sanger wrote "I assert that the hundreds of thousands of abortions performed in America each year are a disgrace to civilization," no religious denomination accepted the practice of contraception. How do you sell the practice of contraception to a public that is totally opposed to it? Well, you sell it to the people by insisting that, with better contraception, there would be less abortion. Today, it is only the Roman Catholic Church that stands for the truth with regard to contraception, yet among its members it is said that 80% practice contraception anyway. Today, American youth are told that the "responsible" thing to do is use contraception, be realistic, and formulate your own values as you go, and, if your contraception fails, get an abortion!

Planned Parenthood is promoting comprehensive health clinics in high schools. With the high rise of teenage pregnancy and AIDS, contraceptives or the availability of contraceptives have done nothing to decrease pregnancies or AIDS. Of 100 couples using condoms to prevent pregnancy, 13 become pregnant within a year. Instead of preventing AIDS, the use of condoms promotes the disease by encouraging sexual activity without providing 100% reliability. AIDS is an equal opportunity infector. It doesn't matter what a person's color, sex, religious convictions, or lifestyle is. Deceiving teens by telling them that they can prevent this and other STD's by using condoms borders on criminality.

Another plague of ignorance that seems to evade education is the thought that anal and oral forms of intercourse are not sex. As a result of the underlying moral climate, children as young as 4th and 5th grades are performing oral sex, especially without much thought about the consequences. These two forms of intimacy are, in fact, sex and can transmit HIV and AIDS as well as other STD's just as easily as vaginal intercourse can.

Sociologically speaking, with the shrinking birth rate (1.8% in the U.S.) and rising elderly population, in the future the work force will not be large enough to support the elderly. We are seeing this already. Thus, there will be a rise in the acceptability of euthanasia. If one can kill before birth, why can't one kill after birth or even during birth (as in "partial birth" abortion). In fact, the majority of abortion clinic doctors are in favor of euthanasia.

Thus, through Margaret Sanger, Planned Parenthood has molded the sexual ethics of the day: Sex is a natural thing for a teenager to desire, and, if a teenager thinks that he or she is to be sexually active, that is his or her decision; all society asks is that he or she not produce children. The message that abortion gives, especially to young people, is that life is not important and that the end justifies the means. It gives them a false sense of liberty without responsibility and the perception that they can establish their own moral code. Abortion is a human issue as well as a moral issue.

"...If we accept that a mother can kill even her own child, how can we tell other people not to kill one another? Any country that accepts abortion is not teaching its people to love but to use any violence to get what they want. This is why the greatest destroyer of love and peace is abortion." Mother Teresa of Calcutta.

History of Church Teaching on Abortion

The Catechism of the Catholic Church states: "Since the 1st Century, the Church has affirmed

the moral evil of every procured abortion. This teaching has not changed and remains unchangeable. Direct abortion, that is to say, abortion willed either as an end or a means, is gravely contrary to the moral law"
(CCC 2271).

In response to those who say this teaching has changed or is of recent origin, here are the facts: From earliest times, Christians sharply distinguished themselves from surrounding pagan cultures by rejecting abortion and infanticide. The earliest widely used documents of Christian teaching and practice after the New Testament in the 1st and 2nd Centuries, the Didache (Teaching of the Twelve Apostles) and Letter of Barnabas, condemned both practices, as did early regional and particular Church councils.

To be sure, knowledge of human embryology was very limited until recent times. Many Christian thinkers accepted the biological theories of their time, based on the writings of Aristotle (4th Century B.C.) and other philosophers. Aristotle assumed a process was needed over time to turn the matter from a woman's womb into a being that could receive a specifically human form or soul. The active formative power for this process was thought to come entirely from the man. The existence of the human ovum (egg), like so much of basic biology, was unknown.

However, such mistaken biological theories never changed the Church's common conviction that abortion is gravely wrong at every stage. At the very least, early abortion was seen as attacking a being with a human destiny, being prepared by God to receive an immortal soul (cf. Jeremiah 1:5: "Before I formed you in the womb, I knew you").

In the 5th Century, this rejection of abortion at every stage was affirmed by the great bishop-theologian St. Augustine. He knew of theories about the human soul not being present until some weeks into pregnancy. Because he used the Greek Septuagint translation of the Old Testament, he also thought the ancient Israelites had imposed a more severe penalty for accidentally causing a miscarriage if the fetus was "fully formed" (Exodus 21: 22-23), language not found in any known Hebrew version of this passage. But, he also held that human knowledge of biology was very limited and wisely warned against misusing such theories to risk committing homicide. He added that God has the power to make up all human deficiencies or lack of development in the resurrection so we cannot assume that the earliest aborted children will be excluded from enjoying eternal life with God.

In the 13th Century, St. Thomas Aquinas made extensive use of Aristotle's thought, including his theory that the rational human soul is not present in the first few weeks of pregnancy. But, he also rejected abortion as gravely wrong at every stage, observing that it is a sin "against nature" to reject God's gift of a new life.

During these centuries, theories derived from Aristotle and others influenced the grading of penalties for abortion in Church law. Some canonical penalties were more severe for a direct abortion after the stage when the human soul was thought to be present. However, abortion at all stages continued to be seen as a grave moral evil.

From the 13th to 19th Centuries, some theologians speculated about rare and difficult cases where they thought an abortion before "formation" or "ensoulment" might be morally justified. But, these theories were discussed and then always rejected, as the Church refined and reaffirmed its understanding of abortion as an intrinsically evil act that can never be morally right.

In 1827, with the discovery of the human ovum, the mistaken biology of Aristotle was discredited. Scientists increasingly understood that the union of sperm and egg at conception produces a new living being that is distinct from both mother and father. Modern genetics demonstrated that this individual is, at the outset, distinctively human, with the inherent and active potential to mature into a human fetus, infant, child, and adult. From 1869 onward, the obsolete distinction between the "ensouled" and "unensouled" fetus was permanently removed from canon law on abortion.

Secular laws against abortion were being reformed at the same time and in the same way, based on secular medical experts' realization that "no other doctrine appears to be consonant with reason or physiology but that which admits the embryo to possess vitality from the very moment of conception" (American Medical Association, *Report on Criminal Abortion*, 1871). Thus, modern science has not changed the Church's constant teaching against abortion but has underscored how important and reasonable it is by confirming that the life of each individual of the human species begins with the earliest embryo.

Given the scientific fact that a human life begins at conception, the only moral norm needed to understand the Church's opposition to abortion is the principle that each and every human life has inherent dignity and, thus, must be treated with the respect due to a human person. This is the foundation for the Church's social doctrine, including its teachings on war, the use of capital punishment, euthanasia, health care, poverty, and immigration. Conversely, to claim that some live human beings do not deserve respect or should not be treated as "persons" (based on changeable factors such as age, condition, location, or lack of mental or physical abilities) is to deny the very idea of inherent human rights. Such a claim undermines respect for the lives of many vulnerable people before and after birth.

Dealing Girls a Raw and Racy Deal

Melinda Tankard Reist, the founding director of Women's Forum Australia, commented that, instead of turning girls into sexual objects, society should teach them to "be resilient and to defend their dignity and self-respect." Tankard Reist is also the author of "*Giving Sorrow Words: Women's Stories of Grief After Abortion*," and "*Defiant Birth: Women Who Resist Medical Eugenics*."

Q: A report published by the American Psychological Association pointed out the damage caused by the sexualizing of preteen and adolescent girls. How serious is this problem today, in your opinion?

Girls are being turned into sexual objects earlier and earlier. The messages they receive through popular culture is that, to be attractive, to be accepted, you have to dress and behave in a sexual manner. There are now lingerie clothing lines for preteen girls, and bras for girls under 10, T-shirts with sexual slogans, and, even, a pole dancing kit complete with a DVD that features "sexy dance tracks" for 6-year-olds.

Popular lines of dolls for girls feature sexy clothing and sexy personas. Gossip magazines aimed at a preteen readership also encourage girls to behave in a sexual manner, with pages devoted to grooming and relationships, even with older men. In advertising catalogues, children are dressed up, made-up, and posed in the same way that adults are. The problem of the premature sexualizing of girls is one of the most serious issues confronting us as a society and suggests that children are interested in, and perhaps open to, approaches for sex.

Young girls are not emotionally equipped to process the sexual messages being targeted at them. It is difficult for them, when abandoned to their autonomy, to resist outside pressure. We are seeing the effects of this premature sexualizing on the bodies of our young women in self-destructive behaviors such as excessive dieting and eating disorders, drug taking, binge drinking, self harm, anxiety, depression, lower academic performance, and ill health. Prescriptions for drugs to treat depression in young girls increase every year. Eating disorders such as anorexia nervosa and bulimia are at epidemic proportions and manifesting in children as young as 8.

Q: Decades ago one of the aims of feminism was to end the exploitation of women, yet contemporary culture has reduced women more than ever to her sex appeal. Has feminism failed women in this area?

I have three daughters, and I see how vulnerable they are to messages about sexuality and body image and how hard it is for them to resist this. It is difficult to raise them in a culture so destructive of their self-esteem and which so abbreviates their childhood. Many gains have been made by the women's movement; that needs to be acknowledged. But, at some stage, efforts to end the exploitation of women were overtaken by the movement for sexual liberalism. Suddenly, women's freedom was reduced to women's freedom to be sexual playthings for male arousal and pleasure. "Liberation" has come to mean a woman's ability to pole dance, expose herself, have multiple partners, and avail herself of cosmetic surgery to enhance her "assets."

Sexual liberalism has not advanced women's freedom but eroded and undermined it. We are living in a sexually brutalized culture. We are seeing more harassment, stalking, and rape, more alcohol-fueled sexual abuse and use of date rape drugs. In general, more predatory behavior.

While radical feminism has questioned the rhetoric of "choice" and exposed the costs to women of the so-called sexual revolution, liberal mainstream "choice" feminism needs to take some responsibility for a confused and destructive notion of freedom that underlines much of the assaults we see today on women's genuine dignity. Ariel Levy's book "*Female Chauvinist Pigs*" describes how a culture of sexual display and raunchy behaviors, i.e. strippers, porn stars, pole dancers, etc., is actually a monoculture that does nothing to empower women. It becomes clear that it is not freedom of expression but a strong cultural expectation for women to appear and behave a particular way.

Q: The unhindered portrayal of sexual images and messages in the media is often defended in the name of freedom of speech. It is also argued that a lack of sexual restraint is "liberating" for women. What is your opinion on these points?

The barrage of sexual images in popular culture cannot be justified on "free speech" grounds when it is causing so much damage to vulnerable children who need protection. Online networks of pedophiles also use "free speech" arguments when trading in images of children being raped.

In Australia, a prominent social researcher, Hugh Mackay, said that there was too much censorship and that no one was harmed by the mere downloading of child porn. He completely ignored the fact that every download fuels a demand for more images and often more degrading images. This attitude also ignores the harm done to the child whose image is used again and again for sexual gratification around the world.

The APA study and other research, for example by the Australia Institute and by my organization, Women's Forum Australia, provides solid evidence for the harm being caused by plastering society's wallpaper with sexual images. What we are witnessing is not liberation but oppression. It is not liberating for young women to be told everyday that their only power is in their sexual currency. It is not liberating to convey to women that their freedom lies in participating in their own exploitation. To portray the sexual as the only value of a woman is oppression.

Q: What are some of the effects have you seen on adolescents and women regarding the consequences of a culture that increasingly puts no limits on sexual expression and behavior?

Young women are facing huge pressure to conform to a sexualized norm. The "norm" is that young women have an insatiable appetite for sex. This is a cultural assumption that women should be having sex at least daily, and something is wrong if they're not. There is profound pressure from the media for young women to be sexually attractive and active. Without this, they are thought of as abnormal and unfulfilled. Young women are compromised by a sexual free-for-all in which they come to expect only cold soulless encounters, where they are always expected to give out sexual favors, with little in return.

The newly released "*Sex lives of Australian Teenagers*" demonstrates this. It makes bleak reading, revealing how little real love there is in the sexual, -- I was going to say "intimate," but there's little real intimacy either -- exchanges between young people.

Q: What can be done to promote a healthier view of women in the sense of a greater respect for their dignity and their role in society?

We need a new strategy for women and girl advocacy. We need to empower young women especially to be resilient and to defend their dignity and self-respect. The decision not to submit to hyper-sexualized messages and to live above the dictates of the culture needs to be seen for what it is, a radical and defiant alternative lifestyle.

Young women deserve better than to be treated as merely the sum of their sexual parts. They need to be given encouragement to develop their minds, their intellects, their deeper inner lives, rather than wasting hours in trying to get their bodies to conform to an idealized, over-sexualized type.

We need more social protection of girls, even more so because of the excesses of popular culture and the sexual danger this puts them in. As Joan Jacobs Brumberg, author of "*The Body Project*," points out: "Although girls now mature sexually earlier than ever before, contemporary ... society provides fewer social protections for them, a situation that leaves them unsupported in their development and extremely vulnerable to the excesses of popular culture and to pressure from peer groups."

We also need to be investing a lot more in raising decent men. There are many men who share the concerns I have raised here. But, there are other men, and it is primarily men, who create the demand for the sort of material that strips women of dignity and respect. It is mostly men who commit sexual crimes, who traffic millions of women and girls a year into the twin industries of pornography and prostitution. It is mostly men who buy pornography and prostituted women. I don't have any easy answers here, but I'd like to know why we aren't doing more to bring out the best, not the worst, in boys and young men. Boys are also demeaned and brutalized by a culture that conditions them to this type of behavior.

In a Melbourne suburb, a group of 12 boys sexually humiliated an intellectually disabled girl and sold the DVD of the abuse to students at high schools in the area for 5 Australian dollars each. The DVD was also shown online for some time before it was removed. But, many people defended their behavior, saying it was just a bunch of boys "having a bit of fun." As long as this attitude prevails, there is little hope for our girls.

We need a new global movement prepared to stand up against corporations, advertisers, the sex industry, the makers of violent video games and demeaning music clips and Internet sites. We need the same momentum as we've seen drive recent movements against global warming and world poverty propel a new movement for fighting our toxic cultural environment.

Moral Evaluation of Human Acts: General Principles

To be able to express an evaluation of human acts in terms of moral good and evil, the person's free will, by which one determines oneself through the choices one makes, must come into play. In fact, morality proceeds from personal freedom, that is, those human acts that, "to the extent that they are deliberate choices,...give moral definition to the very person who performs them, determining his or her profound spiritual traits" (*Veritatis splendor* 71).

Human acts are, thus, taken into moral consideration *insofar as they are deliberate choices*, while influences on freedom are examined at a later point to the extent that they diminish the person's moral responsibility or are a challenge to it.

Every human act must be evaluated first of all on the basis of "objective criteria...criteria drawn from the nature of the human person and of human action (*Gaudium et Spes* 51). It is a question of those "principles of the moral order that have their origin in human nature itself and that concern a person's full development and sanctification" (*Persona humana* 4). In fact, "acting is morally good when the choices of freedom are in conformity with a person's true good," corresponding to the wise design of God and indicated by his commandments that are "a path that leads to life" (*Veritatis splendor* 72).

Now, the moral tradition of the Church, based on the light of Revelation and natural reason, has always stressed unequivocally that "the use of the sexual function has its true meaning and moral rectitude only in legitimate marriage" (*Persona humana* 5). Human sexuality is included in that primordial and good plan of God the Creator, who called man and woman with their reciprocal complementarity to be an image of his own love and responsible collaborators in the procreation of new individuals. Therefore, objective meanings are inherent in the physical acts related to sexuality and represent the norms of conjugal morality. The Second Vatican Council, speaking of the norms of conjugal morality, justified their value precisely as being directed to keeping the exercise of sexual acts within "the context of true love" by safeguarding "the total meaning of mutual self-giving and human procreation" (*Gaudium et Spes* 51)

Through the symbolism of the sexual difference that marks their bodily nature, man and woman are called to achieve two closely connected values: 1) the gift of self and the acceptance of the other in an indissoluble union (one flesh), and 2) openness to the transmission of life. Only in the context of legitimate marriage are these values proper to sexuality adequately respected and achieved. Premarital and extramarital sexual relationships, as well as contraception, are serious violations of these two values.

Only in the conjugal relationship between a man and a woman does their reciprocal complementarity, based on their sexual difference, allow them to become the "one flesh" of a communion of persons who together constitute one and the same procreating principle. The gift of self and the acceptance of the other are real because they are based on the recognition of *otherness* and on the *totality* of the act that expresses them. The gift of the body is a real sign of self-giving at the level of the persons. The meeting of one person with another is expressed with respect for the symbolism of the sexed body. It, therefore, takes place as a true gift of self and as true acceptance of the other. It includes body and soul in a single and intentionally totalizing act. It should be obvious, then, that this gift of self in its totality cannot be accomplished with more than one person, either before marriage or in an adulterous relationship but only in a relationship of total commitment to one person in marriage.

Within the marital union, however, there must be *openness to the procreative meaning* of human sexuality. In the sexual relationship of husband and wife, their bodily act of mutual self-giving and acceptance is ordered to a further good that transcends both of them: the good of that new life that can be born from their union and to which they are called to dedicate themselves. It is the logic of love itself, which requires this further dimension and transcendence without which the sexual act risks turning in on itself by concentrating on a search for pleasure alone and literally sterilizing itself.

Through its openness to procreation, the intimate act of the spouses becomes part of time and history and is woven into the fabric of society. Thus, the use of artificial means of any kind, or any attempt to block the possibility of procreation in any way, is not only a violation of this intimacy, this complete self-giving, but also prevents the Creator from bringing forth new life through the cooperation of the couple as he intended. Contraception, by definition, means "against conception" because a contraceptive is *anything* that prevents the sperm of a man from uniting with the egg of a woman, thus preventing any possibility of "openness to procreation."

Thus, birth control, in reality, is not birth *control* but birth *prevention*. If that doesn't work, it is only a small further step to birth *elimination* through abortion.

--Livio Melina, Professor of Moral Theology, adapted and edited by Patrick J. Hession

A Theological Perspective

Providing a basic plan for understanding this entire discussion is the theology of creation we find in Genesis. God, by his infinite wisdom and love, brings into existence all of reality as a reflection of his goodness. He fashions mankind, male and female, in his own image and likeness. Human beings, therefore, are nothing less than the work of God himself; and, in the complementarity of the sexes, they are called to reflect the inner unity of the Creator. They do this in a striking way in their cooperation with him in the transmission of life by a mutual donation of the self to the other.

In Genesis 3, we find that this truth about persons being in the image of God has been obscured by Original Sin. There inevitably follows a loss of awareness of the covenantal character of the union those persons had with God and with each other. The human body retains its "spousal significance," but this is now clouded by sin.

The Church, obedient to the Lord who founded her and gave to her the sacramental life, celebrates the divine plan of the loving and life-giving union of men and women in the sacrament of marriage. It is only in the marital relationship that the use of the sexual faculty can be "morally good." A person engaging in premarital or extramarital behavior, therefore, acts immorally, at least objectively.

Here, the Church's wise moral tradition is necessary since it warns against generalizing in judging individual cases. In fact, circumstances may exist, or may have existed in the past, that would reduce or remove the culpability of the individual in a given instance; or other circumstances may increase it. What is at all costs to be avoided is the unfounded and demeaning assumption that sexual behavior is always and totally compulsive and therefore inculpable. What is essential is that fundamental liberty characterizes the human person and gives him or her dignity.

What, then, are individuals and couples to do who seek to follow the Lord? Fundamentally, they are called to enact the will of God in their life by joining whatever sufferings and difficulties they experience in virtue of their condition to the sacrifice of the Lord's Cross. That Cross, for the believer, is a fruitful sacrifice since from that death come life and redemption. While any call to carry the Cross or to understand a Christian's suffering in this way will predictably be met with bitter ridicule by some, it should be remembered that this is the way to eternal life for "all" who follow Christ.

It is, in effect, none other than the teaching of Paul the apostle to the Galatians, when he says that the Spirit produces in the lives of the faithful "love, joy, peace, patience, kindness, goodness, trustfulness, gentleness, and self-control" (5:22) and further (v. 24), "You cannot belong to Christ unless you crucify all self-indulgent passions and desires." It is easily misunderstood, however, if it is merely seen as a pointless effort at self-denial. The Cross is a denial of self but in service to the will of God himself, who makes life come from death and empowers those who trust in him to produce virtue in place of vice.

To celebrate the Paschal Mystery, it is necessary to let that Mystery become imprinted in the fabric of daily life. To refuse to sacrifice one's own will in obedience to the will of the Lord is effectively to prevent salvation. Just as the Cross was central to the expression of God's redemptive love for us in Jesus, so the conformity of the self-denial of men and women with the sacrifice of the Lord will constitute for them a source of self-giving that will save them from a way of life that constantly threatens to destroy them.

Christians are called to a chaste life. As they dedicate their lives to understanding the nature of God's personal call to them, they will be able to celebrate the sacrament of Reconciliation more faithfully and receive the Lord's grace so freely offered there in order to convert their lives more fully to his "Way."

The Lord Jesus promised, "You shall know the truth, and the truth shall set you free" (John 8:32). Scripture bids us speak the truth in love (cf. Ephesians 4:15). The God who is at once truth and love calls the Church to minister to every man, woman, and child with the practical solicitude of our compassionate Lord. It is in this spirit that we have addressed this.

--Joseph Cardinal Ratzinger, *Letter to Bishops,* October 1, 1986, adapted and edited by Patrick J. Hession

THE NATURAL FAMILY PLANNING CHALLENGE

There are myths and misunderstandings aplenty when it comes to the Church's teaching on birth regulation. Most ministers, and even many priests, feel a responsibility to tell engaged couples about the good stewardship of using contraception to delay or limit the size of their families. Why, then, does the Church consider contraception a sin? The reason is that contraception prevents a married couple from being fully open to God's gift of children. God is the author and giver of life, which he gives the instant the man's sperm and the woman's egg unite. To block this process through artificial means, or to destroy the sperm and egg after they are joined, is to exclude God's right and participation in the matter of procreation. Usurping his right reduces intercourse to a mere act of pleasure and eliminates the need of responsible stewardship of one's sexuality. By using contraception, men and women can enjoy promiscuity without procreation. Contraception, then, is inherently selfish. On the other hand, according to the experts, the husbands who partner with their wives to use natural, moral methods to plan or space their babies, the truth about natural family planning can transform a man's marriage, life, and faith.

For couples who dare to take the NFP challenge, here are some facts and fictions:

Myth: NFP decreases the chance for a lifelong marriage. Fact: NFP doesn't just increase that chance, it knocks it out of the ballpark. NFP users have a 100 times better chance of staying married than the average American couple. "Once hailed as a boon to marriage, contraception is like a poison that eats away at love. Through contraception, the total self-giving of husband and wife is overlaid by an objective contradictory language. The act says, 'I'm yours,' but, then, you're adding 'except for that [your fertility].' And, things start to deteriorate. When you lie with your body, it is at a level so deep and profound that it will affect everything" (Fr. Richard H. Hogan).

Myth: With its charts and graphs, NFP makes marital relations a clinical exercise. Fact: NFP inspires awe between husband and wife. In NFP classes, "You learn a lot about how ovulation works, how the other forms of birth control work, how they affect the woman, and how they affect the unborn child, and that's a very important thing to me." Bill Johnson. He has learned, for example, that the contraceptive pill not only prevents ovulation but also can cause early abortions after life is conceived. What a man and a woman learn about each other through NFP gives them a glimpse of God. "The man discovers, in a very significant way, some very important hidden aspects of his spouse or his future wife, and she discovers something about him that she didn't know before" (Fr. Hogan).

Myth: NFP harms marriage through lack of physical intimacy. Fact: NFP helps marriage through increased delight in intimacy. According to a Family of the Americas Foundation (FAF) study, a worldwide organization that promotes the ovulation method of NFP, NFP couples have more frequent marital relations than those in the general population. "Contraception diminishes love, and less love means less interest. If sex for pleasure is like dessert, after awhile, how much ice cream can you eat?" (Fr. Hogan).

NFP husbands admit the regular periods of abstinence can be a challenge. But, they say the constraint increases their appreciation for the marital act, making each occasion of embrace like a new honeymoon. In the meantime, they learn to show love in other ways. "Sex is not always just there at the drop of a hat for your own pleasure and your own gratification" (Scott Lash). Bill Johnson cites another unexpected benefit of practicing abstinence through natural family planning. He can make a convincing case for premarital sexual abstinence to his own children, some of whom will soon be teenagers. "It gives me a good feeling to know that I am practicing self-control. In terms of talking with my children, it is not like I'm asking them to do things that I'm not willing to do."

Myth: NFP is only for Catholic couples. Fact: NFP is for anyone who wants to be a better Christian. Rex Moses was a Protestant evangelical who went along with NFP to please his wife. A Baptist, she was not troubled with the moral aspects of birth control but was unhappy with the physical effects. One day, Moses happened upon a newsletter of the Couple to Couple League (CCL), which trains couples in the sympto-thermal method of NFP. Suddenly, Moses said he came to terms with the "profundity of the traditional Christian/Catholic doctrine on contraception." "When I realized virtually all of Protestantism had been washed out to sea [on the issue of birth control]…it caused me to come to grips with the possibility that it is the Catholic Church through which the Holy Spirit has preserved truth."

Myth: NFP users have larger families because the method doesn't work. Fact: NFP users have larger families because they want to. Both NFP and contraception can result in surprise pregnancies, although NFP and hormonal birth control methods like the pill have a better than 97% success rate when used correctly. Yet, compared to the average population, NFP users have larger families. In the FAF survey, three children is the most common number for NFP users, whereas two children is the most common for the average woman. Twice as many NFP users had four children than did the average woman (18% compared with 9%). By its nature, NFP assists couples in being generously open to life. "The self-giving love of husband and wife includes the possibility of children" (Fr. Hogan). But, even when desired, that possibility is not guaranteed. People can actually have a problem, not in thwarting conception but achieving it.

Myth. NFP is only for good marriages. Fact: NFP makes marriages good. There is always hope for a marriage that has started off wrong or gotten off track along the way. "Grace is incredibly powerful here. With God, you make one little baby step, and he's right there next to you. For some people, that step is a huge leap of faith" (Rev. Hogan).

--Ellen Rossini, freelance writer.

Some Protestants find spiritual appeal in natural family planning

Phaedra Taylor abstained from sex until marriage. But, she began researching birth control methods before she was even engaged, and, by the time she married David Taylor, she was already charting her fertility. Taylor, a fresh-faced 28-year-old, ruled out taking birth control pills after reading a book that claimed the pill could, in some cases, make the uterus uninhabitable after conception occurred. She viewed that as abortion, which she opposes. "I just wasn't willing to risk it," she said. Taylor wanted her faith to guide her sexual and reproductive decisions after marriage. Natural family planning felt like the best way to honor God, she said.

The Taylors are one of several couples at Hope Chapel, a nondenominational church where David Taylor, 36, was the arts minister for 12 years, who practice natural family planning. Christian scholars say they may reflect a growing trend among non-Catholic Christians who are increasingly seeking out natural alternatives to artificial contraception. Natural family planning is frequently dismissed by Protestants as an outmoded Catholic practice that most Catholics don't even follow anymore. But, years after Pope Paul VI released Humanae Vitae, the document outlining the church's position on marital sex and procreation, the method and the theology behind it are earning respect among some young Protestants, according to Christian scholars.

The 1968 papal encyclical explains the church's interpretation of the moral and natural laws that includes a prohibition against artificial contraception but allows couples who want to plan their children to "take advantage of the natural cycles immanent in the reproductive system and engage in marital intercourse ... during those times that are infertile." This approach, for years known as the *rhythm method* because it relied on a calendar to track a woman's ovulation based on past cycles, underwent improvements over the years, becoming a more reliable system known as natural family planning.

The natural family planning movement among Protestants is difficult to quantify, but there appears to be growing interest, said the Rev. Amy Laura Hall, a Methodist minister and associate professor at Duke Divinity School. Because she's one of the few Protestant scholars writing about reproductive issues - her latest book is called "Conceiving Parenthood" - Hall frequently fields questions from Christians about family planning at conferences and by e-mail. She said they ask questions like whether it's truly Christian to be preoccupied with finances and getting children into the right schools rather than welcoming children as gifts on loan from God, even if they don't fit into the parents' ideal life plan.

Alexis Dobson, an instructor with the Fertility Care Center of Central Texas, said she's noticed more people who say they are Protestants enrolling in classes, joining the standard flock of Catholic couples required to take at least one class to have a church wedding. Dobson has worked with the Taylors and other couples from Hope, helping them not only avoid pregnancy but achieve conception as well. Usually, she says, women hear about the method from a friend.

That's how it happened for Katie Fox, 31, another Hope Chapel member. After learning about the method from an acquaintance, she researched her options. Before getting married, she took the pill to regulate her menstrual cycle, but she said it had negative side effects. Other forms of birth control such as condoms didn't appeal to her. When she got married, she and her husband used natural family planning.

Fox was raised Catholic but said her mother didn't agree with the Church's stance on contraception. Only after she became an adult and left Catholicism did she begin to appreciate that part of Church teaching, she said. "I feel like it really works in harmony with the way that God designed our bodies to work," she said. "In contrast with the pill, which works by altering and suppressing our natural systems, NFP works by supporting those systems in harmony with their functions. It goes with the flow, so to speak. There is a wisdom and a rightness to that, which I really appreciate." She now is a nondenominational Christian and has a 1-year-old daughter. The method worked, she said, until she and her husband got lazy one month and had sex during Fox's fertile period. Failure rates can be as low as 1 percent but can rise to as high as 25 percent when people do not follow the method perfectly, experts say. But, the pregnancy, she said, helped remind them that God was ultimately in charge.

Megan Tietz, a 31-year-old mother of two who has written about her family planning choices on her blog Sorta Crunchy, said she and her husband also sought to put their trust in God. Although Tietz, a Baptist who lives in Oklahoma, said she doesn't believe today's birth control pill causes abortions, but she does see it as a hurdle to her faith. "The only spiritual objection I have to birth control is that, for me, using hormonal birth control indicates that I don't really trust God with every area of my life," she wrote in an e-mail. "It is an effort on my part to control something that I really believe God can be trusted with."

For David Taylor, the question of how best to faithfully plan families reveals "a fascinating examination of God's sovereignty and human free will." With a pill, he said, people are in control. But, "what does it mean to submit your physical bodies to God's sovereign care? ... God has given us power and freedom to exercise that decision. We can say, 'God, we're going to respect the rhythms you have given us.'" For Phaedra Taylor, avoiding artificial contraception falls in line with her efforts to eat foods that are in season and grown locally and to be a good steward of the Earth. And, they both said the method draws them closer. At a coffee shop near her home in North Austin recently, Phaedra Taylor pulled out a chart covered with an assortment of red, green, and white stickers, indicating when she and her husband can have sex and when they must abstain to avoid pregnancy.

Protestants who choose the natural family planning route often find they are navigating tricky terrain that puts them at odds with older generations and makes them unlikely allies with Catholics. Historically, Hall said, some of the Protestant perspective on contraception stemmed from an antipathy toward Catholic and fundamentalist families.

The Anglican Communion, the worldwide body that includes the Episcopal Church in the United States, lifted the ban on contraception in 1930. In the 1950s, Methodist literature advocated limiting the number of children, Hall said, with the ideal being a two-child, gender-balanced family. Women's rights activists have also supported contraception in previous generations because they believed limiting the number of children would empower women.

Now, as Protestant couples grapple with spiritual questions surrounding reproduction, many are being told by their pastors that they're "crazy or irresponsible to consider not being on the pill," Hall said. That can make it doubly intimidating for a woman to try to explain to her pastor that she wants to follow the rhythm of her body, she said, adding with a laugh, "Protestant pastors are not used to talking about vaginal fluids."

The Taylors agree that Protestant pastors need to generate a more robust discussion about family planning and sex within marriage. "My guess," David Taylor said, "is that most churches are not talking about sexuality."

--Eileen E. Flynn, edited by Patrick J. Hession

NFP Empowers and Liberates

Beatrice Adcock

"Jesus, I trust in you." This is the phrase associated with the increasingly popular devotion to the Divine Mercy. Jesus promises to give us grace for help in daily life in accordance with our degree of trust. How much do we trust, when looking to Jesus in prayer to help us make a generous, yet responsible decision about family planning? Do we take time to inform our conscience on related Church teachings? It is so easy for many to trust our culture instead, with its overwhelming pressure to contracept.

Natural family planning (NFP) is an umbrella term for many methods of family planning which are morally acceptable. Couples are trained to track the menstrual cycle and identify the fertile time, which is about a week. The facts surrounding NFP versus artificial contraceptive use make a compelling argument in favor of trusting Church teaching.

Effectiveness must first be considered. Modern methods of NFP are up to 99.6 percent effective. This is not the old "rhythm method!" NFP methods can also help couples achirve pregnancy. For couples struggling with infertility, Naprotechnonogy-based treatments, which are associated with NFP and aim at identifying and correcting underlying health problems, are between about 38 and 81 percent effective, depending on the cause of infertility. The effectiveness of in-vitro fertilization, which is riddled with ethical problems, significant cost, and health risk, is only between 21 and 27 percent effective.

Another important consideration is health risk associated with hormonal contraceptive use. Side effects range from nausea, headaches, and decreased sexual interest to high blood pressure, depression, and stroke. The World Health Organization has classified oral contraceptives as Group I carcinogens based on strong evidence that they may cause cancer. This is reinforced by several recent studies pointing to the increased risk of pre-menopausal breast cancer in women who have taken oral contraceptives. The most serious risk is not for the woman but for babies she may conceive, as all forms of hormonal contraception and the IUD have the potential of causing early abortions.

By contrast, using NFP gives women valuable health information. The American Academy of Pediatrics and College of Obstrecticians and Gynecologists have called the menstral cycle another vital sign. Health problems can be detected in NFP charts early in their progression, offering the possibility for more effective treatment. A related point is that there are alternatives to the birth control pill for treating common women's health problems such as irregular cycles and heavy bleeding. The pill does not treat the underlying problem, and significant health risks are added.

Other benefits of using NFP include better communication and a lower divorce rate between spouse who are faced monthly with the task of evaluating whether it is a good time for potential conception. Issues in the family, financial, healty, or otherwise, remain on the table and are more quickly resolved. The Church encourages couples to discern, prayerfully and practically, considering their responsibilities. The divorce rate of less than 3 percent among NFP couples is due not only to this healthy communication but also to the respect spouses show each other in cooperating with the woman's physiology. Rather than risking the woman's health for temporary pleasure from contracepted sex, the man is willing to love her unconditionally and exercise self-control. Feminists can jump on a new band-wagon here!

The list of NFP benefits goes on, including environmental respect, shared responsibility for family planning between spouses, the ability to be used in special circumstances, such as after coming off hormonal birth control or having a baby. But, perhaps, the greatest is that just implied: Spouses learn the self-giving and sacrificial love of Jesus! Married couples vow to love that is free, total, faithful, and fruitful. Isn't a contracepting couple that feels the need to use pornography or some other perverse behavior to increase sexual interest enslaved to sexual desire? Or, isn't a couple using a barrier, physical or chemical, or through sterilization, in effect neutering themselves? Are they making a complete gift of themselves in one flesh, imaging God as male and female as Scripture teaches? Do they not, in effect, mock the love that Jesus showed on the Cross and asked us to imitate? The Church is not waging war on women but is standing up in defense of women, offering an option that is empowering, improves marriages, and deepens faith. Women are being liberated, and families are being renewed. In light of the facts, we are encouraged to trust the Church!

Beatrice Adcock is a Registered Nurse and teaches Natural Family Planning workshops.

CHAPTER IV

KIDS AND THEIR TRAINING

Responsibilities toward Your Potential Children - "Children too are a gift from the Lord, the fruit of the womb a reward. Like arrows in the hand of a warrior are the children born in one's youth. Blessed are they whose quivers are full. They will never be shamed contending with foes at the gate" Psalm 127:2-5 (NAB). See your potential children as an asset not as a burden. Plan to enjoy them. They will be gone from you before you know it.

Be constantly aware that your authority over them will be from God, and you will account to him for how you use it. "The Lord honors a father above his children, and he confirms a mother's right over her children" Sirach 3:2. Therefore, parents, "do not provoke your children, or they may lose heart" Colossians 3:21. "Do not provoke your children to anger but bring them up in the discipline and instruction of the Lord" Ephesians 6:4. They will become a reflection and an extension of you.

Discipline - "Folly is bound up in the heart of a child, but the rod of discipline drives it far away" Proverbs 22:15. "Discipline your children while there is hope; do not set your heart on their destruction" Proverbs 19:18. "Train children in the right way, and, when old, they will not stray Proverbs 22:6. "The rod (authority) and reproof give wisdom, but a mother is disgraced by a neglected child" Proverbs 29:15.

King David, who was the greatest King Israel ever had, was not a perfect father. He had a rebellious son, Adonijah, who began to display his ambitions to be king. Yet, "his father had never at any time displeased him by asking, 'Why have you done thus and so?' " 1 Kings 1:5 & 6.

"Discipline your children, then, and they will give you rest; they will give delight to your heart" Proverbs 29:17. "Those who spare the rod (authority) hate their children, but those who love them are diligent to discipline them" Proverbs 13:24.

"If you love your children, you will chastise them often so that you may rejoice at the way they turn out. If you discipline your children, you will profit by them and will boast of them among acquaintances. If you teach your children, you will make your enemies envious and will glory in them among your friends. At your death, you will not seem to be dead, for you have left behind *someone like yourself*, whom in your life you looked upon with joy and, at death, without grief. You have left behind you an avenger against your enemies and one to repay the kindness of your friends.

"If you spoil your children, you will bind up your wounds and will suffer heartache at every cry. An unbroken horse turns out stubborn; an unchecked child turns out headstrong. Pamper children, and they will terrorize you; indulge them, and they will bring you grief. Share not in their frivolity or you will have sorrow with them and, in the end, you will gnash your teeth. Give them not their own way in their youth, and do not ignore their errors. Bend them to the yoke when they are young, thrash their sides while they are still small, or else they will become stubborn and disobey you, and you will have sorrow of soul from them. Discipline your children so that you may not be offended by their shamelessness" Sirach 30:1-13.

Note, this does not give you a license to *abuse* your children. You must know when to stop, and discipline only when you have your own angry *feelings* under control. This is what Paul means when he says, "be angry and sin not."

To sum up, then, "if you have sons, chastise them; bend their necks from childhood. If you have daughters, keep them chaste and be not indulgent to them" Sirach 7:13 & 24 (NAB). "Keep strict watch over a headstrong daughter, or she may make you a laughingstock to your enemies, a byword in the city and the assembly of the people, and put you to shame in public gatherings" Sirach 42:11. "Give a daughter in marriage and you complete a great task; but give her to a sensible man" Sirach 7:25.

RAISING CHILDREN WHO CAN CHANGE THE WORLD

What motivated non-Jews who actively worked to save Jewish lives during the Holocaust to risk their lives while so many others, Christians included, stood by or participated in the Nazi atrocities?

In their book, *The Altruistic Personality: Rescuers of Jews in Nazi Europe* (New York: Free Press, 1992), Drs. Samuel and Pearl Oliner discovered an important fact. The single most important factor in determining whether a person would eventually become a rescuer, a bystander, or a collaborator in the Holocaust was **the parenting style these individuals encountered in their homes as children.**

The following four secrets for raising children who can change the world are gathered from the Oliner's study.

1. **Walk the Walk-** Religious involvement alone was not a significant factor in predicting whether a person would grow up to be a collaborator or a rescuer in Nazi Germany. Many of the collaborators and bystanders were regular churchgoers. Church- going Nazi collaborators were raised in homes in which church was primarily a social activity and faith life had little bearing on "real life." They were the "Sunday Christians" who did not ask what being a Christian meant beyond simply warming a pew on the weekend.

By contrast, rescuers were raised in homes where parents took religious values seriously. They saw their parents making choices in their businesses, social, and home lives that required significant personal and financial sacrifices for the sake of their faith and moral convictions.

If you want to raise truly Christian children, you must ask what your faith requires of you in the home, on the job, and in the community. You must be willing to walk the walk, even when that requires you to make personal, financial, or social sacrifices for the sake of Christ and his church because your children will do as you do, not as you say.

2. **Fathers Must Lead** - Statistically speaking, a significantly greater number of rescuers learned lessons of faith and morality at their father's knee. By contrast, the fathers of bystanders and collaborators left religious training to the mothers, if it occurred at all in the home. The Oliner's study seems to suggest that when fathers are not involved in their children's moral and religious education, even the best efforts of faithful mothers are effectively crippled.

You fathers must take the lead in modeling faith in action and teaching your children the importance of having a personally meaningful relationship with Christ and his church. To do less is to renege on your God-given responsibility to nurture your children's moral character.

If you parents want to raise courageous Christian children, you will do well to remember that mothers cannot do it on their own, even if they have the passive support of their husbands. When it comes to faith and morals, fathers must lead.

3. **Respect the Goodness of Your Children** - Parents of collaborators were significantly morelikely to view their children's misbehavior as a result of innate "badness" or willful manipulation. By contrast, the parents of rescuers tended to view misbehavior as the result of

simple ignorance or clumsy high-spiritedness.

As a result of this difference in parenting philosophies, parents of rescuers tended to respond gently to their children's misdeeds. Over and over, rescuers identified "reasoning" and "explaining" as their parents' preferred intervention. Moreover, children who grew up to be rescuers were rarely, if ever, spanked. This is in contrast to bystanders and collaborators who grew up in homes where corporal punishment (although not necessarily abusive forms of it) was the norm.

The Oliners explained this phenomenon by relying on researcher Dr. Alice Miller's findings that corporal punishment is damaging to a child's will. Early on, a damaged will manifests itself in the form of a very compliant child. As the child matures, he or she lacks the ability to discern between appropriate and inappropriate authority. He or she only knows that he or she must comply with the orders of a superior regardless of what he or she thinks of the orders.

You must emphasize loving guidance with your children, explaining to the degree that they can understand it why certain behaviors or choices are wrong as opposed to merely punishing poor choices. You must gently teach alternatives to unacceptable behavior instead of merely screaming "Stop that!" And, you must use logical consequences, such as requiring your children to clean up their literal or figurative messes instead of heavy-handed consequences that do little but give you a way to vent your anger.

4. **Know the True Meaning of Parental Authority** - While parents of bystanders and collaborators required blind obedience and unquestioning acceptance of parental authority, parents of rescuers practiced Christian authority based on love and service as opposed to mere power. Families are to be communities of love in which parents and children practice a respect for others, a sense of justice, cordial openness, meaningful communication, generous service, a sense of oneness, and all other values that help people live life as a gift.

It was this atmosphere in the childhood homes of rescuers that allowed them as adults to ask intelligent questions about the "authority" (i.e. the Nazis) they were being asked to follow, and instead choose a moral path, often at great risk to themselves.

Likewise, your children need you to base your authority on love, engaging in just, cordial, and loving communication with them. As you do, they will learn to question the conventional wisdom that promotes contraception, abortion, indiscriminate sexual behavior, recreational drug use, and a host of other sinful yet culturally acceptable choices. Ultimately, this dialogue makes the difference between children who will develop faith and morals that will serve them into adulthood and children who simply ride on their parents' coattails until adolescence, at which point they reject not only their parents' authority, but also their parents' beliefs.

If you lead your children, if you men reclaim your moral role as fathers, if you respect the goodness God has created in your children, and if you practice true Christian authority, based on love and service, then perhaps you will have found the secrets to changing the world for and with Christ.

Adapted from an article by Gregory K. Popcak, a Christian psychotherapist and author.

PARENTING STYLES

AUTHORITARIAN PARENTS - Control their children's behavior rigidly and insist on unquestioning obedience. Authoritarian parents are likely to produce children who are withdrawn and distrustful.

PERMISSIVE PARENTS - Exert too little control. Permissive parents are likely to produce children who tend to be overly dependent and lacking in self-control.

AUTHORITATIVE PARENTS - Provide firm structure and guidance without being overly controlling. They listen to their children's opinions and give explanations for their decisions, but it is clear that they are the ones who make and enforce the rules. Authoritative parents are most likely to produce children who are self-reliant and socially responsible.
--Diana Baumrind (1973)

SUMMARY CHART OF FAULTY PARENT-CHILD RELATIONSHIPS

Undesirable Conditions	Typical Effects on Child's Personality Development
Rejection	Anxiety, insecurity, low self-esteem, negativism, hostility, attention-seeking, loneliness, jealousy, and slowness in developing conscience
Overprotection and excessive restriction	Submissiveness, lack of self-reliance, dependence in relations with others, low self-evaluation, some dulling of intellectual striving
Over-permissiveness and indulgence	Selfishness, demanding attitude, inability to tolerate frustration, rebelliousness toward authority, excessive need of attention, lack of responsibility, inconsideration, exploiting of others
Unrealistic demands	Lack of spontaneity, rigid conscience development, severe conflicts, tendency toward guilt and self-condemnation if there is failure to live up to parental demands
Faulty discipline or lack of discipline	Inconsideration, aggressiveness, and antisocial tendencies
Harsh, overly severe discipline	Difficulty in establishing stable values for guiding behavior, tendency toward highly aggressive behavior
Inadequate and irrational communication	Tendency toward confusion, lack of an integrated frame of reference, unclear self-identity, lack of initiative, self-devaluation

The exact effects of faulty parent-child relationships on later behavior depends on many factors, including the age of the child, the constitutional and personality makeup of the child at the time, the duration and degree of the unhealthy relationship, the child's perception of the relationship, and the total family setting and life context, including the presence or absence of alleviating conditions and whether or not subsequent experiences tend to reinforce or correct early damage. There is no uniform pattern of pathogenic family relationship underlying the development of later psychopathology, but the conditions described above often act as predisposing factors.

EFFECTIVE PARENT LEADERSHIP SKILLS

Share Decision Making - When appropriate, share or delegate some of your power and solicit your children's opinions on matters of significance to them, yet, you need to be able to make necessary decisions without consulting them.

Help Your Children Reach Goals - Smooth out the path to reaching their goals, provide necessary resources to your children, ensure that they have proper tools and equipment to accomplish their goals.

Reduce Frustrating Barriers - Help your children cut through red tape when needed, replace faulty equipment, see to it that unsafe conditions are corrected, see that troublesome behaviors are corrected or changed.

Create Opportunities for Personal Satisfaction - Look out for the satisfaction of the whole family and of each of its members.

Exert Influence throughout Other Organizations - Develop clout in terms of getting things done for family members, fight for your children's needs and/or requests that are legitimate.

Provide Emotional Support and Consideration - Engage in activities such as listening to your children's problems and offering them encouragement.

Differentiate Yourself from Your Children - Plan, regulate, and coordinate but do not always become involved in performing your children's work, do personal work like making plans for the family's future, figuring out or managing a budget, etc.

Exercise Appropriate Supervision - Allow your children breathing room in which to carry out their responsibilities, try to avoid suppressing their ideas or creativity.

Establish Realistic Goals - Help your children set goals that will raise both individual and family productivity without developing frustration from not reaching them or excessive pressure to reach them.

Make Your Expectations Known - Make sure each child knows what is expected of him or her in order to contribute to the overall welfare of the family.

Hold Your Child to High, But Not Unrealistic, Standards of Performance - If you expect your children to succeed, they are likely to live up to your expectation.

Give Frequent Feedback on Performance - Tell your children how they can improve and give encouragement for the things they are doing right.

Delegate Assignments to the Right Child - Pass authority down to children as appropriate to their age and ability to assume responsibility now, or willingness to learn, without abdicating your accountability for the outcome.

Manage Crises Effectively - Give reassurance that things will soon be under control, specify alternative paths for getting out of the crisis and choose one of those paths, do not be discouraged or turned aside by obstacles.

THE STAGES OF GROWTH

In 1956, psychiatrist Erik Erikson identified eight stages of development that begin with birth and continue through adulthood. Many mental and behavioral health experts today use these stages as a guide to a person's emotional maturity.

Erikson said that each stage produces its own "psychosocial crisis" and must be learned and resolved before a child can manage the next stage and those that follow it in succession. It is like building a strong emotional house: the foundation must be laid properly before the first floor can be built; the first floor must be structurally sound before the second floor can be built, and so on. People who fail to master a particular stage of development get "stuck" at that stage and cannot move on to maturity. They don't get older, they just get bigger.

The good news is that the stages can be learned at any age. So if your child is stuck, for whatever reason, get help from a mental health professional, Christian if possible.

Stage 1. Learning basic trust. (Hope)

This is the period of infancy through the first one or two years of life. The child who is nurtured and loved develops trust, security, and a basic optimism. Those mishandled become insecure and distrustful.

Stage 2. Learning autonomy. (Will)

Children between 18 months and 4 years old develop a sense of self-possession, initiative, and independence. However, these newly learned traits are usually expressed in a confusing and frustrating way: through stormy tantrums, stubbornness, and negativism. Patience and firm discipline on the part of parents is critical to helping children get through this stage.

Stage 3. Learning initiative. (Purpose)

From about 3 ½ to 5 or 6, children who have a firm grounding in stages one and two learn to imagine, to develop new skills through play, including fantasy, to cooperate with others, to lead and follow. The child who has not successfully negotiated the first two stages will become fearful, socially inept, overly dependent on adults, and restricted in one's scope of play and imagination. This is a good time to introduce children to the wonders of nature and of a God who loves and cares for them. Teach them to care for others and to obey without questioning. They are generally not capable of reasoning, but they can learn to accept proper authority expressed in love. Learning loving discipline helps them to learn later about a God who loves them, even when he disciplines them. They are not "bad persons" but "persons who do bad things (sin) sometimes."

Stage 4. Learning industry. (Competence)

From 5 or 6 through junior high, children are learning to relate with peers according to rules, play with peers in structured activities, master academics and tasks. They increasingly develop self-discipline and industriousness. Distrustful children will doubt the future, and shame and guilt-filled children will experience defeat and inferiority at this stage. This is a good time to teach them the Ten Commandments, and that it is the purpose of the commandments to keep them from hurting others or getting hurt, not to restrict their freedom. This is the purpose of all the rules that you make and the laws that society makes also. God makes rules so that we can be happy and free, not to make us inferior.

Stage 5. Learning identity. (Fidelity)

From about 13 to 20, a person learns how to answer satisfactorily, "Who am I?" But, even the best adjusted adolescents will experience some sense of crisis about role identity. They will try out various roles and personas, experiment with minor delinquency, rebel, and experience self-doubt. Then they move through this to anticipate achievement, a clear sexual identity, and a set of ideals and values that they accept as valid and true for themselves, not because you said so but because they have experienced them as true. Stay close to them and be ready to answer questions and challenges to your (and God's) rules. They need boundaries while they move toward independence so they do not get hurt. Boundaries don't restrict freedom but protect from danger to themselves or to others. Be firm but flexible, and affirm their perfect identity as children of God created in his image, not that of their peers or of society, and brothers and sisters of Jesus, in whom they find their perfect identity.

Stage 6. Learning intimacy. (Love)

Young adults who have made it through the first five stages (with your help and a healthy relationship with you!) can experience true intimacy of the kind that makes committed marriages and enduring relationships with members of both sexes.

Stage 7. Learning generativity. (Care)

Healthy adolescents and adults experience growing pains while learning about parenthood and working productively and creatively.

Stage 8. Learning integrity. (Wisdom)

If the other seven stages have been successfully achieved, the mature adult develops the peak of adjustment: integrity. One understands how to conform sensibly as well as how to create independently. One can be intimate comfortably and is reasonably satisfied with what one has created (children, work, hobbies). If one or more of the other stages has not been resolved, one may view oneself and life itself with dissatisfaction, disgust, and despair.

Helping your children through these stages is a complex and difficult task, but with the help of God, who called you to beget them, it will be a happy and most satisfying work.

Adapted from a Child Development Institute article; www.childdevelopmebnt.info.com

HELPING WITH EXPRESSIONS OF ANGER

Some children and adolescents turn to violence when they feel they can't endure some distressing situation. This is not unusual because it is often the result of frustration that comes from not achieving a perceived need or goal. Children and young people generally lack the skills for expressing their feelings of anger in an appropriate way that doesn't hurt them or others.

These tips may help when you recognize that a child or young person is withdrawing or exploding over everyday frustrations:

- Listen to what the child is saying about his or her feelings and be willing to talk about any subject. Children and young people today are dealing with adult situations, but their minds and bodies are not developed enough to handle these stresses.

- Provide comfort and assurance. Tell the child that you care about his or her problems and show confidence in his or her ability to handle them.

- Tell the child that everyone experiences anger and that it is OK to feel anger. If a person is the cause of the anger, teach him or her to forgive that person as God forgives.

- Teach basic problem-solving skills for use with this or future situations. Then, let the young person use these skills to figure out a solution for himself or herself. Help him or her think about some alternative ways to deal with the cause of the anger.

- Look at how you handle anger. Are you setting a good example?

- Acknowledge good behavior. Take every opportunity to reinforce a child's healthy response to anger.

If a child's angry behavior continues, consult a mental health professional, Christian if possible, for more guidance and helpful resources.

Adapted from The Center for Mental Health Services www.mentalhealth.org/child

INTRODUCING YOUR LITTLE ONES TO GOD AND TO RELIGION

Resources: Handbook of Preschool Religious Education, Religious Education Press, Birmingham, Alabama 1988 Donald Ratcliff, Editor

I Am Special, Our Sunday Visitor, 200 Noll Plaza, Huntington, IN 46750 Joan Plum

The Hurried Child: Growing Up Too Fast Too Soon, Addison-Wesley Publishing, Reading, MA 1981 David Elkind

Never Alone, Joseph F. Girzone, DOUBLEDAY, a division of Bantam Doubleday Dell Publishing Group, Inc. 1994

Research by Toepfer and Epstein: Studied brain growth spurts in the growing child. Their research indicates that the young child grows as the brain increases in size. This would seem to indicate that the youngster is ready for a great deal of learning during the growth spurts. They discovered that between the ages of two and four there is a spurt of brain growth, and that during that time it is appropriate to introduce new concepts.

At four, however, growth slows down, reaching a plateau. Then, if this theory is sound, it might be good for parents and educators to concentrate on reviewing older concepts and waiting to present new materials. The next growth spurt, according to Toepfer and Epstein, occurs at age six.

The danger of "overloading" the young child with learning is very real today. In today's competitive society, too much concern about creating "superbabies" and rushing children through childhood can damage children. Religious educators should resist this trend of overloading children with content.

In "*The Hurried Child,*" Elkind placed the preschool child in the category educators call the ***preoperational period***. Children in this stage of growth (from ages 2 through 6) begin to express themselves in language and also in their abilities to form basic concepts of objects and relationships. Children in these years "become socialized" (Elkind). They also "begin to express fears and anxieties in dreams and symbolic play" (Elkind).

The appropriate starting point for religious training is, therefore, to begin at the beginning - with the creation story. It is the proper place to begin teaching about God. When you teach the creation story, you are teaching that God has done marvelous things. Then, you let them experience it. You bring in fruit from the trees. You let then pet the animals. (Plum)

The latest educational research says that preschool children will learn best if offered the three modes of learning: touching, seeing, and hearing. Kids learn through projects in which they are involved. You can't just read them a story or talk to them. They have to experience the act of sharing, for instance. Then, it has much more meaning (Plum).

The real lessons about God really begin in infancy. The baby's contact with a loving and protective parent or parents begins to teach that life is a gift. The child also learns that he or she is loved and is good. Because preschoolers later learn primarily through experience, a growing understanding of God continues to be closely linked with the child's relationship with parents, family members, and others.

For those reasons, excessive stress on formal preschool religious education could sometimes be off base. Very young children begin to develop attitudes about God, Jesus, and the Church from the family. As parents get ready for church on Sunday or respond to issues in the newspaper or to each other, children will begin to form some kind of attitudes. Concepts really crystallize; they're not handed from a teacher to a child in one day with a particular word. Gradually, in the mind of a child a word like God or Church or Jesus begins to relate to a concept. It might begin with the Christmas celebration in the home or a million other things.

Since concepts continue to "crystallize" in the child's mind, parents and teachers must be careful to present appropriate "food for thought." Despite what many might think, stories from Scripture and even from the Gospels are not always "healthy" for the little preschooler. Three-, four-, and five-year-old lack the ability to interpret in abstract ways. The Gospel was written for adults, and little children have very literal minds.

Parents may teach religion to children. Churches may do the same. But that is not spirituality. That, too, should begin in childhood. Children should be taught about God in a simple, loving way so that they can learn to trust him and to know him as a kind and loving Father who made them, not perfectly but with all they need to grow in his love. They could be taught about Jesus and about his life and how he lived and how he loved people. They could be taught about Jesus as the Good Shepherd who cared for the hurting and the troubled sheep so they can learn to run to him when they have problems and when they fall and make mistakes.

Ordinarily, spirituality is not a child's venture. Spiritual growth, like growth in any other facet of our lives, is a process. It works through phases. The spiritual life is most frequently activated after some personal crisis or tragedy. To force a strong spirituality on children before they are ready is unnatural and can kill a child's interest in religion and, even, in God. We can introduce a child to God and plant the seed that will in God's good time germinate and grow, but moving in a world of spiritual things is not really what interests young people. In fact, it can be harmful to demand too much from them when they are too young to even understand the meaning of the world "spirituality." So many parents, in their excessive zeal to arouse their children's spiritual lives, saturate them with religious activities. When the children become adolescents, they can't stand religion and go to church only after horrendous fights. The older children stop going to church altogether.

Eventually, people come to the realization of their need for God, and their need to grow spiritually. Real spirituality and spiritual growth, however, has to be distinguished from religious activities and pious exercises. Jesus lived for thirty years in Nazareth, and you would think the townsfolk he grew up with would have been impressed with his holiness. You might wonder how Jesus could have kept his exquisite spirituality hidden during all those years so that even his playmates were shocked by his apparent newfound interest in religion. What made it possible for Jesus to keep his spiritual life hidden from the eyes of those who lived so close thim was that his holiness was genuine. It did not depend on showy external practices.

PARENTS' EXPECTATION FORM

Please check the following items that you would like to see changed in your child's behavior.

HOME BEHAVIORS

_____1.   Curfew hours

_____2.   Know exactly where your child is when not at home

_____3.   Clean own room – make bed (if additional work desired, be specific

_____4.   Home for family meals

_____5.   Treat brothers and sisters with respect

_____6.   Help with dishes

_____7.   Take care of trash

_____8.   Control mouth

_____9.   Child's choice of friends

_____10.   Know who child's friends are

_____11.   Other_____

SCHOOL BEHAVIORS

_____1.   Improve attendance

_____2.   Improve school grade performance

_____3.   Show daily homework assignments

_____4.   Do the best they can with the abilities God gave them

CHILD'S EXPECTATION FORM

Please check the following items that you would like to see changed regarding your parents' behavior.

_____ 1.   Parents off my back

_____ 2.   Parents allow more freedom to choose my own friends

_____ 3.   More privacy or free time away from home

_____ 4.   Parents give reasons for decisions

_____ 5.   More freedom to choose my own style of dress and hair

_____ 6.   Parents be honest

_____ 7.   Parents relax

_____ 8.   Parents tell me exactly what they expect of me

_____ 9.   Parents be stricter

_____ 10. Parents talk to me as an adult

_____ 11. Parents trust me

_____ 12. Parents give me credit for the good things I do

_____ 13. Parents set an example

_____ 14. Other_____

GOD'S WORD TO CHILDREN AND YOUTH

"Children, obey your parents in everything for this is your acceptable duty in the Lord" Colossians 3:20. "Obey your parents in the Lord for this is right. 'Honor your father and mother' - this is the first commandment with a promise: 'so that it may be well with you and you may live long on the earth" Ephesians 6:1-3.

"Even children make themselves known by their acts, by whether what they do is pure and right" Proverbs 20:11. "There are those who curse their fathers and do not bless their mothers" Proverbs 30:11. "If you curse father or mother, your lamp will go out in utter darkness" Proverbs 20:20. Therefore, "with all your heart honor your father and do not forget the birth pangs of your mother. Remember that it was of your parents you were born; how can you repay what they have given to you" Sirach 7:27 & 28.

"Listen to me, your Father, O children; act accordingly, that you may be kept in safety. The Lord honors a father above his children and confirms a mother's right over her children. Those who honor their father atone for sins; those who respect their mother are like those who lay up treasure. Those who honor their father will have joy in their own children; when they pray they will be heard. Those who respect their father will have long life; those who comfort their mother obey the Lord. Those who fear the Lord honor their father; they will serve their parents as their masters. Honor your father by word and deed that his blessing may come upon you. A father's blessing strengthens the houses of the children, but a mother's curse uproots their foundations.

"A stupid child is a ruin to a father" Proverbs 19:13a. "Do not glorify yourself by dishonoring your father, for your father's dishonor is no glory to you. My children, help your father in his old age and do not grieve him as long as he lives; even if his mind fails, be patient with him; because you have all your faculties, do not despise him. Kindness to a father will not be forgotten but will be credited to you against your sins; in the day of your distress it will be remembered in your favor; like frost in fair weather, your sins will melt away. Whoever forsakes a father is like a blasphemer, whoever angers a mother is cursed by the Lord" Sirach 3:1-16.

"Let your father and mother be glad; let her who bore you rejoice" Proverbs 23:25. "Those who do violence to their father and chase away their mother are children who cause shame and bring reproach. Cease straying, my children, from the words of knowledge in order that you may hear instruction" Proverbs 19:26 & 27.

"A wise child makes a glad father; a foolish child is a mother's grief" Proverbs 10:1. "A wise child loves discipline; a scoffer does not listen to rebuke" Proverbs 13:1. "A wise child makes a glad father; the foolish despise their mothers" Proverbs 15:20. "Hear, my child, and be wise, and direct your mind in the way" Proverbs 23:19. "Listen, children, to a father's instruction and be attentive, that you may gain insight" Proverbs 4:1. "Hear, my children, your father's instruction and do not reject your mother's teaching; they are a fair garland for your head and pendants for your neck" Proverbs 1:8 & 9.

Finally, "rejoice while you are young, and let your heart cheer you in the days of your youth. Follow the inclination of your heart and the desire of your eyes, but know that, for all these things, God will bring you into judgment" Ecclesiastes 11: 9.

Read the folllowing

DEVELOPMENTAL STAGES

Preschool (1-4 years)

Developmental Tasks: becoming an individual; gaining autonomy; establishing safe separation from parents and other caretakers; physiological stabilization; bonding to one or more parental figures; development of trust and security; exploring one's own environment from a secure place; deepening attachment to caretakers.

Needs/Interests: firm limits and support; secure, patient caretakers; verbal explanations and reassurances repeated; consistent and frequent contact with both parents; routines, help in verbalizing feelings.

Parental Responses: parents should realize that preschoolers need a lot of reassurance backed up by real happenings. They need to see mommy or daddy regularly. Parents should spend a lot of one-on-one time with their preschoolers and reassure them that mommy/daddy love them.

Characteristic Thoughts/Feelings/Behaviors When Parents Separate/Divorce: "Mom/Dad left me" "My family is gone" "Mom's going to leave me too" "I won't ever see Dad again" "Who will take care of me now?"

Danger Signals:

Infancy:

    Sleeping, eating, and digestion problems
    Fretfulness and crying that seems excessive
    Failure to gain weight and to thrive
    Unresponsiveness, apathy
    Seems unreasonably or unpredictably upset by changes in caretakers or environment

Six months to eighteen months:

    Same as above one through four
    Fearful reaction to non-residential parent (indicates lack of attachment)
    Delayed development
    Night terrors

Toddlers:

    Regression - return to safer time
    Developmental lags
    Fear of separation, clinging, whining
    Excessive masturbation
    Excessive aggression
    Frequent and severe temper tantrums

Preschoolers:

    Withdrawal and depression
    Eating and sleeping disturbances
    Crying for long periods after leaving one parent
    Delays in toilet training
    Regressive behaviors - seems to have lost skills previously possessed
    Seemingly very needy for attention, e.g. demanding to sleep with a parent
    Too good, over compliant
    Too serious, emotionally constricted
    Denial
    Inability to concentrate

The preschooler is primarily fearful, confused, and feels guilty. He or she does not really understand what is happening and may feel that one parent is leaving because he or she has been naughty. In terms of behavior, the preschooler may regress and begin bedwetting or day-time wetting; he or she may have difficulty sleeping and/or eating; he or she may wake up often in the night with nightmares. The preschooler may become very aggressive toward age-mates or may become very passive and almost withdrawn. Parents need to reassure them that mommy/ daddy will return regularly and that he/she loves them still.

Early Childhood (3-7 years)

Developmental Tasks: developing initiative; managing impulse; sex role identifications; developing peer relationships.

Needs/Interests: clear parental roles/values; parental cooperation; frequent, continuing contact with the same sex parent; predictable contacts; reassurance of love.

Parental Responses: children in this age group need to be reassured that they are loved by both of their parents.

Characteristic Thoughts/Feelings/Behaviors When Parents Separate/Divorce: "I'm to blame" "I'll get them back together" "I have to choose one parent" "If I don't talk about it, it will be okay."

Danger Signals:

    Increased anxiety, restlessness, over-activity
    Increased moodiness, tantrums, aggression
    School problems - acting out
    Childhood depression, feels rejected
    Denial of all problems
    Intense, one-sided anger at the parent who is blamed for the separation/divorce
    Pseudo-adult, little man/woman role taking
    Somatic complaints
    Increased restlessness
    Phobic fears
    Yearning for absent parent

Passive/aggressive
Low self-esteem

The children from ages five to eight or nine will do a lot of grieving. This age child will cry a lot and seem to be despairing for his or her absent parent. The child is very angry at the residential parent because he or she believes this parent was to blame for the other one leaving. This child also feels that the absent parent must not love him or her anymore because now he or she is gone. Research shows that children at this stage are most likely to believe that something "magical" will happen and mommy and daddy will get back together. They also feel responsible for taking care of their parent whom they see in a tremendous amount of pain.

Children in this age group are most likely influenced by what a parent tells them and seem most likely to be caught in the middle of their parents' battles. Parents need to reassure these children that both parents will still love <u>them</u>, even though the parents may no longer love each other.

Later Childhood (6-12 years)

<u>Developmental Tasks</u>: gaining personal competence; freeing energy from family concerns in order to experience friends, school, industry, and play; developing logical thought; developing a sense of fairness.

<u>Needs/Interests</u>: stability/security at home to free energies; structured schedule; flexibility to allow for social time; lots of explanations; no school changes.

<u>Parents' Responses</u>: the best response to the older child is honesty and that you love and care for him or her. Acknowledge that your child has thoughts and feelings and encourage him or her to talk about them.

<u>Characteristic Thoughts/Feelings/Behaviors When Parents Separate/Divorce</u>: "I'm the only one this has happened to" "I blame Mom/Dad" "Who am I now without my family?" "Who will be in charge here?" "I'm responsible now" "Can I love both parents?"

Included in this group are upper elementary and middle school age children. These children are more likely to understand some of what is happening in their family and why it has happened. In their desire not to make waves, they may deny their own distress. They are anxious at this age to take care of the residential parent and seem to be very sensitive to the anger that that parent may feel toward the other. Researchers show that a small percentage of these children may become an ally to one parent against the other parent. This age group has a tendency to see things as either black or white. These children may be very angry with both parents because of their parents' inability to act appropriately toward the other parent. This age group sees that the children are disciplined for acting inappropriately and selfishly, yet the parents are acting this way themselves.

The older school age child has identity issues at this age as a natural course of development. These issues reach crisis proportions when a separation or divorce is involved. They are unsure of their own identity, and now the family, as they knew it, is no longer the way it was. Children at this age frequent doctors' offices with many physical ailments: headaches, stomachaches, asthma, and even infections. These symptoms can be linked directly to stress reactions.

Parents need to be honest about what is happening, how it will happen (the separation and/or divorce), and how, even though the parents are no longer able to live together, they will still be parents together and still both love and care for the child. Acknowledge that the child's feelings will include anger, and encourage him or her to talk about those feelings.

Be sure to alert the child's doctor and teachers about the changes going on in the family. It will help these important people in the child's life to have some understanding of what may be going on as regards schoolwork and the child's health.

Adolescence (12-18 years)

Developmental Tasks: separation and independence; developing own identity; sexual identity; peer involvement; return to family for emotional refueling.

Needs/Interests: emotional stability/maturity from parents; adequate/flexible parental controls; meaningful contact with parents; low levels of parental conflict and control; consulted, informed, heard; extended times with a parent unnecessary.

Parents' Responses: Honesty is really the best policy with adolescents. They can understand that there are two sides to every story and no one has to put them in the middle. Parents should try to be neither over-protective nor assume that their teenager can cope by himself or herself while the rest of the family members are tended to.

Characteristic Thoughts/Feelings/Behaviors When Parents Separate/Divorce: "I'll act mature to cope" "Why can't my parents get it together?" "My parents' separation/divorce is no big deal" "If I accept step-mom (dad), Mom (Dad) will be mad" "I'm jealous of Dad's girlfriend" "Mom's dating is gross!" "Am I loveable?" "Will I get divorced someday?"

Danger Signals:

> Withdrawal from the family; perhaps withdrawal from peers
> Intense feelings of loss, helplessness, low self-esteem, depression, suicidal thoughts or feelings
> Uncontrollable anger and/or violence toward a parent
> Promiscuity
> Manipulation of one parent against another
> School problems - failure, truancy
> Substance abuse
> Pseudo-maturity for control
> Involvement with antisocial activities
> Denial
> Pessimism for own lovability in the future
> Competition or over-identification with parent

The adolescent, ages 13-18, is more developed intellectually and socially and, therefore, is probably better equipped to handle the separation/divorce at least as a life event. However, this age group is also very good at masking true feelings and acting as though they have it all under control. The teenager can see his or her parent's pain and doesn't want to add to it. He or she feels that parents should take care of themselves and that younger siblings and the teen can make do. What happens, however, is that adolescence is a time when children need consistency and discipline. With parents out of control, many teenagers are left to their own devices. Some just become adults quicker; others do not know what to do with their own feelings of anger and hurt, and they begin to act out. This can be a time when teenagers experiment with alcohol/drugs, promiscuity, and other types of inappropriate behavior.

The adolescent may have difficulty forming intimate relationships because of what he or she sees as failure when one trusts enough to marry and the marriage falls apart. Others will rush into marriage to escape the home situation or to prove that they can make it work. Still others are searching for the closeness that they feel they lost with their parents' separation/divorce. Teenagers should be given access to both parents at their discretion and allowed to develop and maintain a relationship defined by them and each of their parents independently of the other.

Adult Children (18-death)

Developmental Tasks: establish one's place in the world; contribute to the well-being of society.

Needs/Interests: to be kept out of the middle, maintenance of the family hierarchy and parental responsibility.

Characteristic Thoughts/Feelings/Behaviors When Parents Separate/ Divorce: "If I go to Dad's house for Thanksgiving, Mom will feel rejected" "I'll avoid both of them."

THE LIMITS OF PARENTHOOD

I gave you life but cannot live it for you.
I can teach you things but cannot make you learn.
I can give you direction but cannot be there to lead you.
I can allow you freedom but cannot account for it.
I can take you to church but cannot make you believe.
I can teach you right and wrong but cannot decide for you.
I can buy you beautiful clothes but cannot make you beautiful inside.

I can offer you advice but cannot accept it for you.
I can give you love but cannot force it upon you.
I can teach you to share but cannot make you unselfish.
I can teach you respect but cannot force you to show honor.

I can advise you about sex but cannot keep you pure.
I can tell you about the facts of life but cannot build your reputation.
I can tell you about drink but cannot say 'NO' for you.
I can warn you about drugs but cannot prevent you from using them.

I can tell you about magnificent goals but cannot achieve them for you .
I can teach you about kindness but cannot force you to be gracious.
I can warn you about sin but cannot make you moral. --Author Unknown

CHAPTER V

CLEANING OUT THE COBWEBS

God's love is manifested in many ways in the world and in your life: healing, provision of your needs, peace in your heart, answers to your prayers, and so forth. But, there are two primary manifestations of his love that God wants you to experience in your life and in your marriage, and then to share with those with whom you come in contact. These are *giving* and *forgiving*.

If God had not given, you would not know true love. Love is expressed in giving. Giving is expressed in service. Jesus said that he did not come to be served but to serve and to *give* his life as a atonement for sin. The ultimate goal of God's sending of his Son is to make you at-one (at-one-ment) with him though the forgiveness of your sins.

So, *forgiving* is the other manifestation of God's love for you. Forgiving simply means to *give before*: *fore*-give. Before you even asked, God the Father fore-gave you through the death of Jesus Christ.

However, it is important and necessary for you to acknowledge your sins and faults to him and to ask for his forgiveness to be applied to you. "If we say that we have no sin, we deceive ourselves, and the truth is not in us. If we confess our sins, he who is faithful and just will forgive us our sins and cleanse us from all unrighteousness. If we say that we have not sinned, we make him a liar, and his word is not in us" 1 John 1:8-10. "But, if anyone does sin, we have an advocate with the Father, Jesus Christ the righteous, and he is the atoning sacrifice for our sins, and not for ours only but also for the sins of the whole world" 1 John 2:1b & 2.

The Father wants you to forgive in the same way and with the same attitude as Jesus forgave you. "Whenever you stand to pray, forgive anyone against whom you have a grievance so that your heavenly Father may in turn forgive you your transgressions" Mark 11:25 (NAB). This is particularly true of your potential spouse and/or children.

Note, you are to forgive your potential spouse and others even before or whether they ever ask you for forgiveness. And, even if they never admit any offense against you. "If you forgive others their transgressions, your heavenly Father will forgive you. But, if you do not forgive others, neither will your Father forgive your transgressions" Matthew 6:14 & 15 (NAB).

Are you, then, to do nothing to the person who offends you even if it is your potential spouse or other family member? Yes, if possible. "If your brother or sister sins, you must rebuke the offender; and, if there is repentance, you must forgive. And, if the same person sins against you seven times a day and turns back to you seven times and says, 'I repent,' you must forgive" Luke 17:3 & 4. This is exactly the way Jesus and the Father forgive you, no matter how often you sin, as long as you truly turn back to him (repent) and ask for forgiveness.

What are some clues as to whether you are forgiving or not? Whether you are cleaning out the cobwebs in your life? Well, the opposite of forgiveness is unforgiveness. Ask the holy Spirit to search your heart for anything that your potential spouse has done to you that you have not yet forgiven. Remember, forgiving means giving-before. If you are waiting for your potential spouse to ask for forgiveness, you need to fore-give. Your potential spouse may not even know that he or she has done anything that needs to be forgiven. Or, maybe he or she just didn't know what he or she was doing or that it was hurting you. It may be necessary for you to express to your potential spouse when and how he or she has sinned against you. Gentle confrontation in love will bring correction, repentance, and healing to your relationship.

When you have deliberately sinned against your potential spouse, it is important for you to ask for forgiveness. Mutual forgiveness will bring tremendous freedom to your marriage because it will keep your relationship open and honest before each other and before God.

Finally, it is extremely important that you forgive yourself when you have done anything wrong. If you have trouble doing so, remember this: if almighty God can forgive your sins and faults, it is the utmost of arrogance to say that you cannot forgive yourself!

What are some other clues that you haven't forgiven yourself, your potential spouse, or others? One is *hurt* and *anger*. With whom are you angry? Who has hurt you or is hurting you? Your parents, relatives, friends, boss or co-worker, someone at church, your Pastor or other Minister, yourself, God? Yes, it is possible to get mad at God! Go ahead and admit it! After all, he made you and knows all about your weaknesses. That is why he sent Jesus, you know!

Another indication of unforgiveness, and probably the most destructive, is *bitterness* and *hatred*. Are you harboring bitterness or hatred against anyone? Even your potential spouse? Even God? Clue: who is the object of your blame?

Love is manifested in *giving* and *forgiving*. If you abide in giving and forgiving, you abide in God, and he will abide in you and in your marriage. And, your sins will be forgiven.

What human nature does is quite plain, says St. Paul (Galatians 5:12-21). Mark says that all evils come from within people, from their hearts, and they defile (Mark 7:21-23). "Once in a while, it is good for you to have a dress rehearsal of the day when you will stand before the Lord." (A Pastor in India). This means coming into his presence as if you were standing before the judgment seat of Christ, where there is no hiding or pretence. Ask him to help you see your heart as he sees it. When he reveals it to you, be willing to humble yourself and respond, "Father, I have sinned."

Quietly examine your conscience, using those sins defined in the following pages. Confess those in which you are or have been involved. Confession is simply agreeing with God to the truth of what you have done. Repent of them by turning away from them. Ask forgiveness specifically for any sin you have committed that the Father brings to your mind through the holy Spirit and ask him to forgive you and wash you clean by his precious blood. This will give the Holy Spirit freedom to make your heart soft toward God, and you will be amazed by the blessing and grace he will pour out on your life as a result. Any of these sins that you do not confess, renounce, repent of, and have forgiven, however, will remain cobwebs in your life, will be destructive of yourself, and will continue to hinder your relationship with God and with your mate.

Forgive yourself for committing these sins. Forgive each person that comes to mind as having sinned against you and give that person or situation over to God. In this way, you will clean out the cobwebs in your life and in your marriage. Then, go free in your spirit to let the Bond of unity-in-love, the Holy Spirit, join you and your spouse in a new and ever deeper love that reflects the Trinity as Family in your marriage as God so greatly desires and as the world so desperately needs.

Sins That Defile

Here are some particular texts of Scripture that spell out, in some detail, what acts will exclude us from the kingdom of God, if not repented from.

"From within people, from their hearts, come evil thoughts, unchastity, theft, murder, adultery, greed, malice, deceit, licentiousness, envy, blasphemy, arrogance, folly. All these evils come from within, and they defile" Mark 7:21-23.

"Do you not know that the unrighteous will not inherit the kingdom of God? Do not be deceived, neither fornicators nor idolaters nor adulterers nor boy prostitutes nor practicing homosexuals nor thieves nor the greedy nor drunkards nor slanderers nor robbers will inherit the kingdom of God" 1 Corinthians 6:9 & 10.

And, as Paul often does, he repeats what is particularly important for us to understand: "For you were called to freedom, brothers and sisters. Do not use this freedom as an opportunity for the flesh but, rather, serve one another through love....Now the works of the flesh are obvious: immorality, impurity, licentiousness, idolatry, sorcery, hatreds, rivalry, jealousy, outbursts of fury, acts of selfishness, dissensions, factions or party spirit, envy, drinking bouts, orgies, and the like. I warn you, as I warned you before, that those who do such things shall not inherit the kingdom of God" Galatians 5:13, 19-21.

We also find this clear warning in Ephesians: "Be sure of this, that no immoral or impure or greedy person, that is, an idolater, has any inheritance in the kingdom of Christ and of God. Let no one deceive you with empty words since it is because of these things that the wrath of God comes upon the disobedient" Ephesians 5:5-6.

And, again, in the book of Revelation: "Blessed are they who wash their robes so as to have the right to the tree of life enter the city through its gates. Outside are the dogs, the sorcerers, the unchaste and fornicators, the murderers, the idol worshipers, and all who love and practice deceit Revelation 22:14-15.

Fornication - In the Old Testament fornication referred to any form of idolatry or worship of idols. It often involved sexual intercourse with temple prostitutes, both female and male, particularly young boys. Currently, it means sexual intercourse, including oral or anal intercourse, between a male and female of any age, neither of whom is married.

Wicked Designs, Evil Thoughts, or Evil Ideas against another person or persons.

Theft - an act or instance of stealing.

Murder - the unlawful killing of one human being by another, especially with premeditated malice. It includes abortion and "mercy killing."

Adultery - voluntary sexual intercourse or activity between a married person and a partner other than the lawful spouse.

Greed or **Covetousness** - an excessive desire to acquire or possess, as wealth or power, beyond what one needs or deserves.

Maliciousness or **Malice** - a desire to harm others or to see others suffer.

Wickedness - viciousness or depravity in word or action.

Deceit - the act or practice of causing a person to believe what is not true. It involves falsehood or the deliberate concealment or misrepresentation of truth with the intent to lead another *who has a right to know* into error or into disadvantage.

Sensuality or **Impurity** or **Unchastity**- excessive devotion to gratification of the physical appetites, especially the sexual appetite.

Licentiousness - lack of moral discipline or sexual restraint; no regard for accepted rules or standards.

Indecency - offensiveness to good taste or public moral values.

Envy or **Jealousy** - a feeling of discontent and resentment aroused by another's desirable possessions or qualities accompanied by a strong desire to have them for oneself.

Blasphemy - a contemptuous or profane act, utterance, or writing concerning God; claiming for oneself the attributes or rights of God; speaking of God or something sacred in an irreverent or impious way.

Slander - utterance of defamatory statements injurious to the reputation or well being of a person; a malicious statement or report.

Arrogance or **Pride**- over-conviction of one's own importance; haughty self-importance; an excessively high opinion of oneself; conceit.

Foolishness or **Folly**- lack of good sense or judgment, lack of understanding or foresight.

An obtuse spirit - lacking keenness or quickness in comprehending or discerning.

Lewd conduct - preoccupation with sex and sexual desires; lustfulness.

Immorality - actions contrary to established moral principles.

Filthy Actions - actions or language considered obscene, immoral, or obsessively concerned with matters of a sexual nature or with an obsessive interest in sex.

Idolatry - the worship of an image or other material object representing a deity to which religious worship is addressed; blind adoration of, reverence for, or devotion to any person or thing, e.g. movie, rock, or sports star; material possessions.

Sorcery or **Witchcraft** - the art, practices, or spells of one supposed to exercise supernatural powers through evil spirits; magic, especially black magic, in which supernatural powers are exercised through the aid of evil spirits. The art or practices of a witch, whether white or black. It includes also consulting psychics, astrology, ouija boards, and other means of divination.

Hostilities or **Hatreds** or **Rivalry** - animosity, ill will, unfriendliness, antagonism, feelings or conditions of hostility, hatred, or bitterness.

Bickering or **Strife** - engaging in petulant arguments, quarreling, conflict, or discord.

Anger or **Outbursts of rage** - a revengeful passion or emotion directed against one who inflicts a real or supposed wrong.

Selfishness - self-seeking, egotism.

Ambitiousness - excessive desire to obtain power, superiority, or distinction.

Dissension - violent disagreement or discord.

Factions or **Party Spirit** - party strife or intrigue, often using unscrupulous methods to accomplish selfish purposes.

Drunkenness or Drinking Bouts - a willful loss of control over physical or mental powers by means of alcoholic liquor, a drug, or other substance.

Orgies or **Carousing** - wild, drunken, or licentious festivities, parties, or revelry; any proceedings marked by unbridled indulgence of passions; secret rites or ceremonies connected with the worship of evil spirits or Satan celebrated with wild dancing and singing, drinking, drugs, or sexual excesses.

Practicing Homosexuality - acts or practices between or among members of the same sex.

A CELEBRATION OF RECONCILIATION

"Our Father in heaven, hallowed be your Name"

PRAISE AND THANKSGIVING

I praise you, Lord.
I sing for joy to you, O God, who protect me.
I come before you with thanksgiving
and sing joyful songs of praise.
For you, O Lord, are a mighty God -
a mighty King over all the gods.
You rule over the sea, which you made;
the land also, which you made;
I bow down and worship you;
I kneel before you, Lord, my Maker!
You are my God.
I am the one you care for, for whom you provide.
I will listen today to what you say.
Psalm 95:1-7

Praise the Lord, my soul!
All my being, praise his holy name!
Praise the Lord, my soul,
and do not forget how kind God is.
You, O God, forgive all my sins
and heal all my diseases.
You keep me from the grave
and bless me with love and mercy.
You fill my life with good things
so that I stay young and strong like an eagle.
I was on my way to Hell, but you restored my life.
You have changed my sadness into a joyful dance.
You have taken away my sorrow
and surrounded me with joy
so I will not be silent;
I will sing praise to you.
Lord, you are my God;
I will give you thanks forever.
Psalm 30:1-3, 11-12

I praise you, Lord, because you are good.
I sing praise to your Name because you are kind.
You, my God, are great, greater than all the gods.
You do whatever you wish in Heaven and on earth,
in the sea and in the depths below.
You bring storm clouds from the ends of the earth,
you make lightning from the storms,
and you bring out the wind from your storeroom.
You, Lord, will defend me. You will take pity
on your servant.
Psalm 135:3, 5-7, 14

I thank you, Lord, with all my heart;
I sing praise to you before the gods.
I bow down and praise your name
because of your constant love and faithfulness,
because you have shown that your name
and your commands are supreme.
You answer me when I call to you;
with all your strength you strengthen me.
Even though you are so high above,
you care for the lowly,
and the proud cannot hide from you.
When I am surrounded by troubles,
you keep me safe.

> You oppose my angry enemies
> and save me by your power.
> You will do everything you have promised.
> Lord, your love is eternal.
> Complete the work you have begun.
> Psalm 138:1-3, 6-8

> I am like an olive tree
> growing in your house, O God.
> I trust in your constant love
> forever and ever.
> I will always thank you, Lord,
> for what you have done;
> in the presence of your people
> I will proclaim that you are good.
> Psalm 52:8 & 9

"Your Kingdom come, your will be done on earth as in heaven."

ACCEPTANCE OF GOD'S WILL

Lord, it is your will
- to show mercy to whomever you choose, to have pity on whomever you wish.
- to destroy the wisdom of the wise and to thwart the cleverness of the clever.
- to bring to light what is hidden in darkness and to manifest the intentions of hearts.
- to put your law in our hearts and to write them on our minds.
- to draw close to us as we draw close to you.
- to dwell with us and walk among us, to be our God and for us to be your people.
- to refresh all who are weary and find life burdensome, if they come to you.
- for those who do the will of the Father to enter the Kingdom of God.
- to pour out a portion of your Spirit on all mankind.
- that not a single one of your little ones shall ever come to grief.
- to never desert us nor forsake us.
- that we grow in holiness, that we abstain from immorality, and that we refrain from overreaching or cheating our brother or sister.
- for us to rejoice always, to never cease praying, and to render constant thanks.
- to hear us when we ask for anything according to your will.
- for us to be obedient to every human institution.
- that those who suffer as your will requires continue in good deeds and entrust their lives to you, a faithful Creator.

> You, O Lord, are King.
> You are clothed with majesty and strength.
> Your throne, O Lord, has been firm
> from the beginning,

and you existed before time began.
Psalm 93:1 & 2

"Give us today our daily bread."

PETITION AND INTERCESSION

Lord, you are my Lord.
All good things I have come from you.
You, Lord, are all I have,
and you give me all I need,
My future is in your hands.
How wonderful are your gifts to me,
how good they are.
I praise you, Lord, because you guide me,
and in the night my conscience warns me.
I am always aware of your presence.
You are near, and nothing can shake me.
And so I am thankful and glad
and feel completely secure
because you protect me from the power of death.
The one you love you will not abandon
to the world of the dead.
You will show me the path that leads to life.
Your presence fills me with joy
and brings me pleasure forever.
Psalm 16:2, 5-11

Have pity, O Lord, on your servant.
Fill me each morning with your constant love
so that I may sing and be glad all my life.
Give me now as much happiness
as the sadness you allowed me
during all my years of misery.
Let me, your servant, see your mighty deeds.
Let my descendants see your glorious might.
Lord, my God, may your blessings be with me.
Give me success in all I do!
Psalm 90:13-17

***"Forgive us our sins as we forgive those
who sin against us."***

ACKNOWLEDGMENT OF SINFULNESS

Lord, I look up to you,
up to Heaven where you rule.

As a servant depends on his master,
as a maid depends on her mistress,
so will I keep looking to you,
O Lord my God,
until you have mercy on me.
Be merciful to me, Lord, be merciful.
Psalm 123:1-3

Lord, you examine me and know me.
You know everything I do;
from far away you understand all my thoughts.
You see me, whether I am working or resting;
you know all my actions.
Even before I speak,
you already know what I will say.
You are all around me on every side;
you protect me with your power.
Your knowledge of me is too deep;
it is beyond my understanding.
Where could I go to escape from you?
Where could I get away from your presence?
If I went up to heaven, you would be there.
If I lay down in the world of the dead,
you would be there.
If I flew away beyond the east
or lived in the farthest place in the west,
you would be there to lead me,
you would be there to help me.
I could ask the darkness to hide me
or the light around me to turn into night,
but even darkness is not dark for you,
and the night is as bright as the day.
Darkness and light are the same to you.
You created every part of me;
you put me together in my mother's womb.
I praise you because you are to be feared;
all you do is strange and wonderful.
I know it with all my heart.
When my bones were being formed,
carefully put together in my mother's womb,
when I was growing there in secret,
you knew that I was there --
you saw me before I was born.
The days allotted to me
had all been recorded in your book
before any of them ever began.

O God, how difficult I find your thoughts;
how many of them there are!
If I counted them,
they would be more than the grains of sand.
When I awake, I am still with you.
Examine me, O God, and know my mind;
test me and discover my thoughts.
Find out if there is any evil in me
and guide me in the everlasting way.
Psalm 139:1-18; 23 & 24

Be merciful to me, O God,
because of your constant love,
because of your great mercy.
I have been evil from the time I was born;
from the day of my birth I have been sinful.
Sincerity and truth are what you require;
fill my mind with your wisdom.
Create a pure heart in me, O God,
and put a new and loyal spirit in me.
Give me again the joy
that comes from your salvation
and make me willing to obey you.
Then I will teach sinners your commands,
and they will turn back to you.
My sacrifice is a humble spirit, O God;
you will not reject a humble and repentant heart.
Psalm 51:1, 5 & 5, 10, 12 & 13, 17

You forgive me, Lord,
so that I should reverently obey you.
I wait eagerly for your help,
and in your word I trust.
I wait for you, Lord,
more eagerly than watchmen wait for the dawn --
yes, than watchmen wait for the dawn.
Psalm 130:4-6

*"Do not subject us to the final test
but deliver us from the evil one."*

PROTECTION and DELIVERANCE

Lord, hear my prayer!
In your righteousness listen to my plea;
answer me in your faithfulness!

Don't put me, your servant, on trial;
no one is innocent in your sight.
I lift up my hands to you in prayer;
like dry ground my soul is thirsty for you.
Answer me now, Lord!
Don't hide yourself from me.
Remind me each morning of your constant love
for I put my trust in you.
My prayers go up to you;
show me the way I should go.
I go to you for protection, Lord;
rescue me from my enemies.
You are my God; teach me to do your will.
Be good to me and guide me on a safe path.
Rescue me, Lord, as you have promised;
in your goodness, save me from my troubles!
Because of your love for me,
kill my spiritual enemies
and destroy all my oppressors
for I am your servant.
Psalm 143:1 & 2, 6 & 7, 8-12

My help comes from you, Lord,
who made Heaven and earth.
You will not let me fall;
you, my protector, are always awake.
You will guard me;
you are by my side to protect me.
The sun will not hurt me during the day,
nor the moon during the night.
You, O Lord, will protect me from all danger;
you will keep me safe.
You will keep me as I come and go,
now and forever.
Psalm 121:2 & 3, 5-8

Lord, how happy is the person you instruct,
the one to whom you teach your law!
You give me rest from days of trouble.
You will not abandon me;
you will not desert me
because I belong to you.
I said, "I am falling,"
but your constant love, O Lord,
held me up.

Whenever I am anxious and worried,
you comfort me and make me glad.
You, O Lord, defend me;
you, my God, protect me.
Psalm 94:12-15, 18 & 19, 22

CONCLUDING PRAYER

Lord, make me an instrument of your peace.
Where there is hatred, let me bring love.
Where there is injury, pardon.
Where there is doubt, faith.
Where there is despair, hope.
Where there is darkness, bring your light.
Where there is sadness, bring your joy.
Divine Master, grant that I may not seek so much
To be consoled as to console,
To be understood as to understand,
To be loved as to love.
For it is in giving that I receive,
It is in pardoning that I am pardoned,
It is in dying to self that I am born to eternal life.
--St. Francis of Assisi

www.ingramcontent.com/pod-product-compliance
Lightning Source LLC
Chambersburg PA
CBHW081132170426
43197CB00017B/2838